Rescued!
401(k) Plan Traps
Business Owners
Must Avoid and Fix

by Andrew Dickens

TABLE OF CONTENTS

DISCLAIMERS

This publication contains the author's opinions and is designed to provide accurate and authoritative information concerning Company Sponsored Retirement Plans. It is published with the understanding and intent that neither the author nor the publisher are in any manner offering accounting, tax, legal, financial planning or investment advice or any other form of professional services. The accounting, tax, legal, financial planning and investment information presented in this publication have been checked with sources believed to be reliable. However, all material in this publication may be affected by changes in the laws or in the interpretations of such laws since the manuscript for this publication was completed. For these reasons the accuracy and/or completeness of such information and the opinions based thereon are subject to change at any time. In addition, state and local laws or procedural rules may have a material impact on the general recommendations made by the author and the strategies outlined in this publication may not be suitable for specific legal entities or individuals. The author and publisher expressly disclaim any responsibility for any loss incurred as a result of any actions, investments or planning decisions made by the reader. The reader must seek the services of appropriate licensed and qualified professionals to obtain current and accurate accounting, tax, legal, financial planning and investment advice.

FOREWORD

Government regulations are increasing in number and their liberal (ab)use applied to business owners. While discussing the risks inherent in "Qualified Retirement Plans" (QRPs) -- as those in the industry describe 401(k), 403(b), 401(h), 412(i) parts of the Internal Revenue Service (IRS) code, and more -- with a prominent attorney whose firm may have been at risk for violating conflict of interest rules in its own QRP, he dismissed the risks as only theoretical.

Not long afterward, on February 19, 2011, the front page of the Times and the Wall Street Journal described that the Supreme Court now made it a reality to be able to sue your employer sponsored QRP. What was once "theoretical," now was reality.

The Department of Labor (DOL) has the capacity to "attach" the full net worth of the QRP "sponsor," also known as the business owner. And it is highly likely the DOL can and will pierce any asset protection or estate planning or business planning veil too. There is no place to hide from them.

Some of the most respected and well-known companies were recently sued, were forced to disgorge large amounts of cash. Forbes on August 15, 2014 ran an article entitled "Why your 401(k) is Worth Suing Over."

That is why I encouraged Andrew Dickens to write this book. He is clearly ahead of the curve as one of America's leading authorities on retirement plans and how dysfunctional and dangerous they may be to business owners of this great land. And he provides real solutions to protect you and your employee-"plan participants".

That is why I encourage you to peruse this book for the highlights. This trickle down regulation and lawsuit is probably coming to a business near you. Don't get caught in the snare. Andrew outlines the problems and the solutions.

Life gets ever more complicated. This book brings some simplification without being simplistic. It can help you avoid the problems, and reduce the liability. And help you make more money at the same time.

Happy Planning,

Mitch Levin, MD, CAPP, CWPP
CEO Summit Wealth Partners, Inc.

PREFACE

In just the last few years, some of the largest investment companies and vendors in the retirement plan industry have been sued by their own employees for breach of fiduciary responsibility with regards to their own retirement plans and investments.[1] These are the very same companies you might entrust to service your own plans. Accusations typically revolve around excessive fees paid by participants, conflicted or poor investment options, employer stock, and other areas of mismanagement or failures of oversight.[2]

The risk of both litigation and regulatory enforcement action is greater than even before. You need to read this book because it has already happened to some of the "expert" companies who service the industry, and thus it can happen to you. And thanks to renewed efforts by government regulators to enforce the Affordable Care Act, the number of auditors in this space is greater than ever before and they are looking for violations in both healthcare and retirement plans.

This book was written to show you how to lower your costs, improve management and performance, and what to look for in experts to assist you along the way. We will jump start your understanding of

---

1   Brown, Andy. (2014). *Chefs Who Don't Eat Their Own Cooking*. Retrieved from Brown Wealth Management, LLC: www.brownwm.com/chefs-dont-eat-cooking/

2   The Oyez Project. (2009). LARUE v. DEWOLFF, BOBERG & ASSOCIATES, INC. Retrieved from The Oyez Project at IIT Chicago-Kent College of Law: www.oyez.org/cases/2000-2009/2007/2007_06_856

what you need to know to run a cost effective, properly managed retirement plan while minimizing your liability exposure and keeping you under the radar of the auditors. The ultimate goal is to have a properly managed, effective plan that provides a valuable benefit for your employees and keeps you out of the crosshairs of government regulators and ambitious attorneys.

I wrote this book for you because experience has repeatedly demonstrated to me that most employers understand very little about what it means to sponsor a retirement plan, and consequently most of the time they don't come close to getting it right. The proof is in the pudding: **over 70% of plans audited by the Department of Labor are found to have violations that result in fines, restitution, or both** and the financial consequences are very often paid personally by the individual(s) responsible for that aspect of the plan.

While risks certainly exist as in any venture, this should not deter you in offering these plans to your employees. In fact, the risk your employees face of not having enough money saved to replace a portion of their income significant enough to maintain their standard of living are *many times greater* than the risk you face of being fined or sued over the retirement plan. Tax efficient savings options for employees are minimal in absence of a company sponsored retirement plan, and helping your employees get to retirement comfortably will increase your productivity while decreasing the expenses and liabilities associated with an aging workforce that *won't* retire because they *can't* retire.

A properly managed retirement plan with good design, effective education, and prudent back-end policies, processes and procedures will almost assuredly provide a valuable recruiting and retention tool while minimizing the risk of litigation or regulatory enforcement. Despite best intentions, too many retirement plan sponsors are not equipped with the knowledge or support to maximize efficiencies and synergies while minimizing liabilities. With this book, I hope to elevate your knowledge and put you in a position to manage your plan with the best practices in the industry.

My goal in writing this is to provide the small business owner with a base of knowledge so that you can competently engage other service providers and know that everyone is "speaking the same language". You will get a clear, concise, and uncomplicated explanation of what your responsibilities are to a retirement plan as the sponsoring employer.

We will encompass both entry level material as well as more complex subjects, with good substance and actionable items to get you doing what the best managed plans in the business are doing. Each section is dedicated to a specific area of plan governance that is critical to understand yet often misunderstood.

At the beginning of selected sections, I will relate an experience that correlates to the subject matter (names are omitted and relevant information has been altered to protect the identities of the subjects). I'm going to use as little industry jargon as I can, and whenever I can't I'll try to explain before I use it. I'm also going to try to leave out much of the legalese associated with this topic but retirement plans are governed by a set of laws that in some opinions *harbor the strictest and highest standards of any set of laws in the entire country*; so some cursory immersion into legal references will be inevitable.

This book is designed for use by sole owners, partners, boards, and committees; essentially any entity offering or considering offering a "defined contribution" (401(k)) or "defined benefit" (pension) plan for their owners and employees will find value in this book. However this is not meant to be the comprehensive, all-encompassing guide requiring several thousand pages. Instead this is something you will be able to read in a couple of days at your convenience.

Unless the plan's sponsoring employer is an expert in plan governance, fiduciary requirements, and the nuances of the law, **it is critical to have a competent, trusted advisor and/or legal counsel to assist the sponsoring employer with understanding the roles and responsibilities of retirement plan management.** Many advisors, agents, brokers and

CPAs only dabble in retirement plans incidentally to the course of their other business. We continue to see plans that are severely underserved by these professionals who receive compensation from the plan while providing very little effort supporting the plan sponsor needs, and in some cases giving just plain bad advice, if any at all. I'll speak more on this at the end of the book.

If you have gotten this far, you should pat yourself on the back. This is not the type of reading material that most people are going to casually pick up. Most likely you've had an experience, or know someone who has, that's taken you down the road of exploring whether what you are doing is right, how to correct the things that need to be fixed, and what can happen if you ignore it.

I will make you three promises:

1. I'm writing this book with the interests of the employer at heart;
2. I'm going to try and make this as light a read as possible;
3. And I guarantee you'll find at least several actionable items that will help drive your plan's performance and protect you in the process.

And I'll make every effort to be available to answer your questions to the best of my time and ability.

Finally, this is the first edition of this book. As time passes and rules changes, I'll keep updating as need be. With that being said, the information contained herein should not be taken as legal, tax or accounting advice. Your particular facts and circumstances may affect any action or outcome, so please consult with an appropriate professional before acting on any of the information in this publication.

And finally, if you want to contact me for any reason, from just a question to needing genuine assistance, you can reach me at the following:

- Email: adickens@mysummitwealth.com

- Phone: (407) 656-2252 x1000

- Mail: 800 N. Magnolia Ave. #105
            Orlando, FL 32803

INTRODUCTION:
THE ROLE OF COMPANY
SPONSORED RETIREMENT PLANS

THE STORY...

I'm relating this story because it made such an impression on me that it eventually changed the entire focus of my business, and made me as committed as I am today to this subject.

My first year in this business I received a call from Jim, an existing client of our firm, requesting a review of his investments. I had previewed his accounts, (formerly the responsibility of another advisor who had recently taken an opportunity at a competitor) and noticed his age, totality of his portfolio, and the notes left by the previous advisor relating to his retirement objectives. Jim was a retired business owner and I noticed immediately that his portfolio was relatively small considering these factors. But like many other clients, I suspected that he had not been entirely forthcoming with his previous advisor regarding all of his assets.

Jim was a "country boy"; an elderly gentleman with southern manners and hospitality. His wife Theresa was a dedicated mother (now grandmother) and had never worked outside the home. After spending a few minutes getting to know each other, I inquired as to his previous occupation. He was the former sole owner of a commercial transportation company, and had been retired for about ten years.

When I asked him about his exit from the business, I learned that he had suffered a life changing medical event that forced him into retirement. This event cost him a substantial amount of after tax savings he had accumulated due to inadequate medical coverage and other issues with the health insurance provider. Jim was completely unprepared to exit his business, but acting on the best instructions from his doctors he decided it was time to hang it up.

Like many business owners, the majority of his net worth was tied up in the business. Jim was unprepared to sell his business and was now confronted with the need to sell it quickly. Despite the fact that an asset sale was a very reasonable means to exit, he was committed to his many long standing employees and didn't want to see them suddenly unemployed. So he arranged a management buyout with his existing key employees. Unsurprisingly the buyers were unable to finance the entire purchase, so Jim agreed to a down payment with a long term earn out option.

Through a series of unfortunate events, including a claim against the company a few years after the buyout, Jim only received two full payments and a subsequent partial payment before the company became insolvent. His investment accounts were all non-qualified (after tax). When I asked him what happened to his qualified accounts, I learned he had never had a properly constructed retirement plan other than a small contributory Roth IRA.

As it turned out, he had not been hiding other assets from his former advisor as I suspected. This once successful, hardworking husband and father had been reduced to surviving off a pittance compared to his former successes. And although he weathered the most recent financial crisis due to mostly conservative investments, Jim was struggling to maintain what little of his former lifestyle was left, and he was deeply concerned about what would be left for Theresa who was almost sure to outlive him.

As I listened and sympathized with this family, it dawned on me that this former business owner exited his business to reduce his stress and was now succumbing to stress. This was not a family enjoying the little things in life comfortably. It was unfortunate that we didn't meet sooner so that I could have helped him implement a well-structured, properly managed exit strategy that included a tax qualified company sponsored retirement plan.

After this meeting, I committed myself to learning and helping others avoid the same mistakes that this unfortunate but well intentioned businessman made. I am on a mission to help you avoid his same fate or worse.

✻✻✻

In order to understand the role that a company sponsored retirement plan can play, it's important to understand a little about the history of retirement in the United States, why a company would want to take on the responsibility of offering a retirement plan, and important things to consider before making that decision. The goals of this section are to:

- ✓ Introduce you to the evolution of retirement in the United States;
- ✓ Understand the "disconnect" between savings requirements and realities;
- ✓ Determine the reasons for sponsoring a retirement plan;
- ✓ Define ERISA and Title I retirement plans;
- ✓ Warn you of potential problems when multiple business interests are at play;
- ✓ And define the Six Core Elements of any successful retirement plan.

The Concept of Retirement

We are in an interesting time in the brief history of retirement plan evolution. There was a time not so long ago (less than a century ago), when the concept of "retirement" had no tangible meaning for most. To most people retirement was something that happened when you could no longer provide for yourself or the people you love. People worked to provide sustenance and shelter. Once the body broke down, you relied on family or the generosity of others to survive.

Most of the modern world began to see a shift in the perception and realities of retirement around the beginning of the last century. In the United States, the "First and Second Deals" by FDR, which included the implementation the Federal Deposit Insurance Corporation (FDIC), and later Social Security among other socio-economic reforms, paved the way for a means to accumulate and distribute income that provided independence and security for millions of working Americans. To a financial advisor like me, retirement today means "the cessation of earned income".

Today, government sponsored entitlement programs such as Social Security and Medicare offer substantial benefits for retirees, but the amount of benefit available has been slowly declining over the years and will be difficult to predict in the years ahead.

Retirement Income Sources

Retirees are concerned with many factors, not the least of which is where their income will come from. Retirees often face a daunting dilemma: how to liquidate assets into an income stream over an unknown time frame, since we cannot predict when or how death will occur. Retirees who are fortunate enough to live long lives in retirement face other considerations as well, such as the long term effects of inflation, interest rate variability, market volatility, taxes and healthcare costs.

Advances in healthcare are increasing life expectancies, and with extended care options (assisted living and nursing homes) many retirees may find themselves living twenty, thirty or even forty years without any earned income. Often there is little left to plan for the next generation's inherited wealth, unless the retiree did an exceptionally good job saving, investing, and living off of that savings (AND was lucky not to have any major medical or long term care needs).

Income sources for retirees generally come from a few sources: social security, pension income, pre-tax savings, after-tax savings, and occasionally business or real estate interests. We are going to touch on social security and savings options, as these are the primary resources for most retirees.

Social Security

The premise behind Social Security as it exists in its current form is to supplement retirement income by means of lifetime payments from a trust whose assets come from payroll reductions of all contributors. One must earn enough "credits" to qualify and earnings (indexed for inflation) are counted towards the benefit. There is a benefit and payroll deduction ceiling for high income earners.

Early access to retirement benefits (prior to "Full Retirement Age") reduce that benefit for life, whereas delayed access increases it significantly. It's an annuity payment where those who die early without receiving much if any benefit are subsidizing for those who live beyond their life expectancies. Much of the growth and expansion of benefits, including disability, Medicare and cost of living adjustments (COLAs) took place through the early 1970's. Nevertheless, Social Security was only designed to provide for partial retirement security, with the remaining coming from worker's savings. Despite its intended design, Social Security is the mainstay of retirement income benefits for *too many* Americans today.

Benefits are based on indexed earnings counted over the highest 35 years of earnings, and earnings amounts are capped for the purposes of determining benefits (in other words, there is a limit to how much you can collect). Currently, taxes against social security income depend on the Modified Adjusted Gross Income (MAGI for short, which counts back tax-exempt interest into your Adjusted Gross Income):

- For single filers with less than $25,000 MAGI, no part of social security income is counted for tax purposes;

- For single filers with a MAGI greater than $25,000 but less than $34,000, 50% of social security income is counted for tax purposes;

- For single filers with a MAGI of $34,000 or higher, 85% of social security income is counted for tax purposes;

- For married couples filing jointly, the lower threshold is $32,000 and the higher threshold is $44,000, but the percentage of social security income counted for tax purposes is the same in each threshold;

- These numbers are currently fixed and not inflated for earnings purposes.[3]

Proper social security planning can reduce taxable income in retirement, even for high income earners. Often post retirement income earners in higher tax brackets will delay social security benefits as long as possible, preferring to take income from other sources prior to filing for social security benefits to take advantage of reduced taxable income in later retirement years.

Currently the social security fund is under pressure due to an aging work force, disability benefits and inflationary pressures. While social security benefits are currently indexed for inflation annually, the income thresholds for taxation of benefits is fixed ensuring that more benefits will be taxable in the future. Additionally, measures have been implemented (such as chain CPI indexing) or considered being implemented (such as increasing the full retirement age or means testing for higher income earners) to reduce or limit benefits for future generations, making it difficult to estimate benefits for younger workers.

The Birth of the Pension Plan

By the end of the Second World War, industrial manufacturing experienced a boom because factories which were making planes, ships, tanks, jeeps, guns, ammo and bombs for the war were reconfigured to produce consumable goods and vehicles. Men returning from

---

3   Internal Revenue Service. (2014). *Are Your Social Security Benefits Taxable?* Retrieved from IRS: www.irs.gov/uac/Newsroom/Are-Your-Social-Security-Benefits-Taxable

war needed employment, and the industrial complex had prospered enough to facilitate the mass production of consumables at relatively inexpensive costs because the facilities and processes were mostly established as a result of the war effort.

The abundance of labor, combined with the subsequent economic boom, resulted in companies providing new types of benefits for retirement: the defined benefit plan, otherwise known as the pension. Companies set aside money to provide specific benefits for workers upon retirement. These benefit pools were managed, operated, and invested by the company for the workers' benefit. The company had the ultimate responsibility to fulfill the obligations promised under the pension plan.

The Death of the Pension Plan

The rise of labor unions created greater pressure to increase benefits. Concessions were made that were too generous and relied on suspect accounting and actuarial methods. The result was many industries were hammered by insufficient returns, and corporate profits shrunk as companies tried to save the plans by sinking more money into them and renegotiating benefits. The airline and automobile industries were particularly hit hard.

Companies found themselves on the hook for these benefits, and many corporations became insolvent trying to keep up. As a result, companies looked for ways to provide these benefits while minimizing their liabilities. Corporate America wasn't the only one on the hook; the U.S. government was realizing they had a sustainability problem too. The 1970s and 1980s saw systematic reductions in social benefits, and then the corporate sponsored defined contribution plan was born.

Instead of the company promising a specific benefit at retirement and financially obligated to see it through, numerous other arrangements began to become commonplace. The end result is something of a combination of different efforts, but for the most part today's defined contribution plan is a plan where the participant's elective payroll deferrals are invested in financial instruments that the participant often but not always controls. Success or failure of these plans is defined by how much benefit they can provide and for how long, and the onus lies on the employees to save enough and invest smartly. The corporation no longer has the liability of guaranteeing a specific benefit.

Although this created a much better arrangement for corporate America, these types of plans varied wildly in form and function. A number of infamous defaults with defined benefit plans and discriminatory and inconsistent benefit and vesting schedules with defined contribution plans resulted in Congress seeing fit to enact legislation to protect the already vulnerable worker from rapidly evolving complexity and abuse of corporate retirement plans.

The Employee Retirement Income Security Act of 1974

ERISA stands for The Employee Retirement Income Security Act[4]. ERISA is federal law that governs all pension and welfare benefit plans in the United States, with some very limited exceptions. Enacted by Congress in 1974, ERISA was created to protect the interests of plan participants and beneficiaries by requiring standards of conduct by fiduciaries, disclosures to participants, and providing remedy through the courts[5].

ERISA is the main source of governing law regarding retirement and welfare benefit plans today, and ERISA has a specific definition of fiduciary that applies to plans covered under the law that is the source of great confusion; we'll be taking steps to clarify this later.

---

4   Employee Benefits Security Administration. (n.d.). *The Employee Retirement Income Security Act (ERISA)*. Retrieved from United States Department of Labor: www.dol.gov/compliance/laws/comp-erisa.htm

5   Legal Information Institute. (n.d.). *29 U.S. Code § 1001 - Congressional findings and declaration of policy*. Retrieved from Cornell University Law School: www.law.cornell.edu/uscode/text/29/1001

The Gap

Today, retirement income planning is a critical component of financial planning. So why is it that most Americans are woefully unprepared to retire? There are several reasons we can ascribe this to:

• Many Americans are dependent on Social Security because they either didn't save, or didn't save enough (social security was never designed to provide more than one third of retirement income);

• Lack of access to professional guidance;

• Saving too little and/or too late;

• Lack of access to retirement plan vehicles;

• Medical expenses before or after retirement;

• Inflation;

• Investment behavior;

• Taxation of retirement investment accounts.

Advances in modern medicine now have pushed life expectancies well beyond what the social systems, which are meant to stabilize the lifestyles of older Americans, are able to sustain. As we are aging, we are putting more stress on a system that will not be viable in its current form. Unless we start taking control of our futures, the medical and financial burdens of the aging population, which is currently experiencing a "boom," will crush these programs under its weight. But for our purposes, let's explore what options are available for workers to save for retirement with no access to workplace retirement plans.

The Workers' Savings Options

In addition to social security, the average American worker with no access to pensions or other workplace retirement plans has two savings options: pre-tax and after tax savings. After-tax savings are generally invested in savings and brokerage accounts, with taxation of investment performance running concurrently as gains or income are realized. This is an inefficient form of savings due to the heavy burden of taxation, but the introduction of the Roth Individual Retirement Account (Roth IRA) has helped with the deferral of taxes on the investments and tax free access for qualifying withdrawals due to the ability to withdraw qualified contributions and investment returns tax-free.

A big drawback to the Roth IRA is that your annual contribution is limited to $5,500 (2014) or $6,500 if you are over the age of 50, AND if your combined modified adjusted gross income is over a certain limit (married filing jointly was $181,000 for 2014) you enter a contribution "phase out" with incomes over a slightly higher amount (married filing jointly was $191,000 for 2014) completely ineligible to contribute.[6]

As opposed to Roth IRAs, pre-tax savings allow for reduced taxable income in the form of deductions for contributions, with tax deferral of investment performance. Withdrawals from the account are treated as taxable income. However, pre-tax investment vehicles (also known as "tax qualified plans", "qualified plans", or "qualified retirement plans") that are not part of a corporate sponsored retirement plan are very limited in form and function.

Individual Retirement Accounts (IRA) are generally the only form of pre-tax savings allowed for typical wage earners outside employer sponsored plans (self-employed individuals have other options). The contribution limits are the same as the Roth IRA; in fact, they are the combined limits (you cannot contribute the maximum amount to each plan in the same year, but rather contribute to one or the other or split the $5,500/$6,500 maximum over each plan).[7]

---

6   Internal Revenue Service. (2014, Feb). *Roth IRAs*. Retrieved from IRS: www.irs.gov/Retirement-Plans/Roth-IRAs

7   Internal Revenue Service. (2014, Oct). *Retirement Topics - Contributions*. Retrieved from IRS: www.irs.gov/Retirement-Plans/Plan-Participant,-Employee/ Retirement-Topics-Contributions

The premise behind pre-tax savings with fully taxable distributions is that when in retirement taxable income will be lower due to no earned income, distributions from "non-qualified" accounts, and social security benefits. This also relies on the assumption of no increases in tax brackets and lower income needs in retirement. For highly compensated wage earners, there is a real risk that their income needs in retirement could be taxed as much or more than they would have been while working. Therefore it is critical to diversify your retirement vehicles as much as possible, allowing you to pull income from different buckets at different times based on the circumstances.

How Much Should We Save?

These projections vary from person to person, but let's consider a 30 year old married couple with a combined taxable income of $100,000 per year in 2014 and no retirement savings. And let's assume that they plan on working for 40 more years, until age 70 when they might be eligible for social security. They want to live off of HALF of their combined income in retirement, or $50,000 of taxable income (and half of their current income is probably an unrealistically low estimation as most people will need between 60-80% of pre-tax retirement income to maintain their lifestyle). How much do they need to save? Let's use some ballpark math to figure this out:

1. WHAT IS THE PURCHASING POWER OF THEIR DESIRED INCOME AT RETIREMENT?
We need to calculate what the purchasing power of $50,000 is 40 years from now. So if we assume inflation remains at long term historical levels of 3.5%, we would then expect the purchasing power to be reduced by half every twenty years; therefore in 40 years they'll need $200,000/year to be able to have the same purchasing power that $50,000 has today.

2. HOW LONG WILL THEY NEED THAT INCOME?
Let's assume that at least one of them may live until age 90. That's 20 more years after retirement at which time that $50,000 in purchasing

power in retirement will only provide the purchasing power of $25,000 at age 90 without cost of living adjustments for inflation. We'll continue to adjust for inflation during retirement since we're expecting to live another 20 years.

3. HOW MUCH WILL SOCIAL SECURITY PROVIDE?

Tough question, because we don't know what form SS will have 40 years from now. For sake of argument let's assume they'll receive a combined social security income of $30,000 today, and let's inflate those 40 years from now but at half of the rate than inflation to be conservative. That would be $60,000 in retirement. So the grand total of replacement income will be $200,000-$60,000 = $140,000/year.

4. HOW MUCH CAN THEY WITHDRAW TO MAKE IT LAST THAT LONG.

Let's assume they want to leave nothing for their children in their retirement accounts, spending down the account to almost nothing after 20 years of retirement (which also means we must hope to die at age 90 as planned). First, we need to know how much the investments will earn in retirement. Let's assume a conservative and stable return of 5% during retirement. In order to spend down our retirement assets in 20 years, they'll need to take about 7% withdrawals net of earnings, which amount to 12% per year (about 3-4 times what a financial advisor would recommend). Let's say they listen to their advisor and cut that number in half to 6%, in case one of them lives an additional ten years.

TOTAL SAVINGS GOAL = APPROXIMATELY $2,333,000.00

5. HOW MUCH DO THEY NEED TO START SAVING NOW?

First we need to know how much the investments will earn pre-retirement. Let's assume a higher return of 7%. Finally breaking out a calculator, we find that they will need to save about $1000 per month, or 12% of their current $100,000 income, for the next 40 years to get them at or past the goal of $2.3 million in retirement savings.

Now the limitations of this scenario are too numerous to list, but we've taken a simple example and arrived at a number that is generally consistent with what experts are saying today: most people will need 60-80% of their pretax income to maintain their lifestyle in retirement, and thus people need to be saving between 10-20% of their current pre-tax income. Since this example uses only 50% of pre-tax income, the estimated savings goal of $2.3 million may be conservative.

The Disconnect From Reality

Given the contribution limits for individual retirement plans, a gap exists between how much pre-tax income can be saved and what typically should be saved. An individual Retirement Account allows for $5,500 per year (2014) in contributions per individual under the age of 50 ($6,500/yr over 50). Thus, married couples can only contribute $11,000 per year towards their pre-tax retirement plan.

The impact is noticeably worse for highly compensated persons. Consider the previous example, but for a couple with pre-tax earnings of $300,000. There is no way that contributing $11,000 to IRA accounts for both spouses before age 50 ($13,000 after age 50) will come close to bridging the retirement income gap. The remainder would have to consist of after tax savings, and given the high tax bracket the couple is in, the effect of taxes on savings can be substantial. In effect, there is a "reverse discrimination" against highly compensated earners. Something better must be available, and in fact there is.

The Employer Sponsored Retirement Plan

An employer sponsored retirement plan is simply a retirement plan made available by an employer, regardless of incorporated status. These plans take many forms, from discretionary profit sharing arrangements to hybrid defined contribution-defined benefit plans. The important thing to know is that employer sponsored retirement plans generally offer higher contribution limits than individual plans. But they come with their own set of disadvantages too. We're going to explore options, benefits and drawbacks in greater detail soon enough.

Why Should I Offer a Retirement Plan?

Company sponsored retirement plans are important in attracting and retaining top talent. These plans offer contribution maximums far beyond what an employee can contribute in a traditional or Roth IRA, making their value as part of a retirement savings strategy critical when savings rates for most people should be between 10-20%. Aside from being an attractive benefit to help attract and retain talented employees from your competitors, company sponsored retirement plans also offer significant benefits for business owners.

Foremost, a retirement plan adds diversification to a business owner's net worth. Usually a large percentage of an owner's net worth is in the value of the business. A financial advisor would tell you that "the preponderance of your wealth is tied up in a single, illiquid micro-cap stock whose value may fluctuate based on your health and work performance;" certainly a violation of several basic saving and investing principles.

In addition to increasing diversification, other benefits of retirement plans typically include:

• Tax deferral of investment gains;
• Creditor protection;
• Reduced taxable income based on current contributions;
• Reduced payroll taxes.

Many businesses are reluctant to implement a retirement plan because of the perceived costs and administrative headaches. Teaming with the right service providers and advisors will certainly help alleviate the administrative burdens, and with proper plan design the tax savings alone are often more than enough to cover the administrative costs associated with the retirement plan.

TRAP #1

NOT IDENTIFYING THE GOALS OF THE BUSINESS WHEN DECIDING TO OFFER A RETIREMENT PLAN

Unfortunately, too many business owners make the decision to implement a retirement plan without taking the time to determine what the goals of the plan are for the business, ownership, key personnel, and rank and file employees. Careful consideration of what you want the plan to accomplish is the first step to implementing a meaningful plan in line with corporate objectives.

Questions to Ask Yourself Prior to Sponsoring a Plan

An employer needs to think seriously about what you want the plan to accomplish. Consider the following questions:

- What do you want the plan to achieve for you, your family, and your partners?

- What do you want the plan to achieve for top management and/or key personnel?

- Do you want to maximize benefits for the owners, top management and/or key employees?

- What do you want the plan to achieve for the rank and file employees?

- Do you want to achieve the goal of getting all your employees to retirement?

- Do you want the plan to be attractive for recruiting and retaining management and employees?

- How much money are you willing to contribute to setup and administration?

- Are you going to make contributions on behalf of employees?

- Are your cash flows stable or will you need flexibility for making contributions?

- How much do you want or need to save for yourself?

These are just a few of many questions you should be asking yourself before and after sponsoring a retirement plan. As advisors, our job is to help you setup and design a plan that meets the particular needs of your business. Offering a retirement plan just as a fringe benefit with little consideration for what you want the plan to achieve will produce just as little in the way of results for you, your employees, and the business. So think carefully on what you want the plan to achieve for everyone involved.

Qualified and Non-Qualified Plans

There are two distinct types of retirement plans available for employers to sponsor: the "qualified" plan and the "nonqualified" plan. Qualified plans are plans with preferential tax treatment, specifically pre-tax contributions and tax deferral on growth for the participant, and tax deductible matching or discretionary contributions by the employer.

The majority of qualified plans are bound by ERISA, with exceptions for certain tax-exempt, government and some religious institutions. ERISA has established requirements for vesting schedules, contribution limits, and nondiscrimination for rank and file employees. Qualified plan assets are required to be segregated from the general assets of the sponsoring company and are generally exempt from the claims of creditors.

Non-qualified plans are plans that are not afforded the same tax treatment as qualified plans; nor are they genertally bound by ERISA but instead by the Internal Revenue Code, and in particular IRC section 409A. Non-qualified plan contributions are generally not tax deductible to the employer until "constructive receipt" by the beneficiary, at which time they are taxable to the employee.

There are certain rules required by section 409A, but the biggest advantage of non-qualified plans is absolute discretion with regards to who can participate. These plans are generally known as "top hat" or "golden handcuff/parachute" plans, due to their use primarily with high compensated individuals. Non-qualified plan assets are held in the general accounts of the employer, and subject to all indebtedness and claims of creditors by the same.

This book will dive into the details of plans that are governed only by ERISA.

ERISA and Title I

ERISA is broken up into four titles, but for our purposes we're only going to briefly discuss the first title, Title I. Title I: "Protection of Employee Rights", lays out the groundwork for most of the operational considerations in modern retirement plans. The U.S. Department of Labor has primary responsibility for reporting, disclosure and fiduciary requirements; and the IRS has primary responsibility for participation, vesting and funding issues. However, the U.S. Department of Labor may intervene in any matters that materially affect the rights of participants, regardless of primary responsibility.

Title I also prescribes which plans are under its jurisdiction. Plans not covered under Title I include plans offered by entities of government, certain exempt churches, certain excess benefit plans defined in the code, workman's compensation/disability plans, and a few others.

For the employer in the United States, you should consider any retirement benefit plan to be covered under Title I unless you are absolutely certain otherwise. The aforementioned "non-qualified" plans, which are unfunded (meaning the benefit pool remains as part of the general assets of the employer until constructive receipt by the beneficiary) is an example of a retirement benefit plan NOT covered under ERISA Title I.

TRAP #2

NOT IDENTIFYING CORPORATE STRUCTURES OR RELATIONSHIPS THAT CAN CAUSE PLANS AND POTENTIALLY ELIGIBLE EMPLOYEES TO BE TIED TOGETHER

Certain relationships or corporate structures can cause unintended consequences for retirement plans that, if not identified early, can create significant problems for the plan and its sponsor. This is particularly true for mergers and acquisitions, or new business ownership interests by certain owners, and should be evaluated continuously even if no complications exist at the beginning. Even a spouse's outside business ownership interests need to be considered.

Warning – Unintended Consequences

At all times before and during plan sponsorship, sponsoring employers need to be aware of certain control issues that can cause a plan to be required to cover employees of other entities. The question involves "control groups" and "affiliated service groups". Plan sponsors need to coordinate carefully with a skilled advisor and/or third party administrator to ensure that no problems arise due to ownership of other entities or close affiliations with service groups. Business interests of family members can influence the result of these tests. Some questions to ask yourself:

- Do you own any other business interests, regardless of form or industry?

- Do you provide services closely with any other business entities?

- Do you have any direct lineal or spousal family members with ownership of any business, regardless of form or industry? [8]

The technicalities involved in determining whether a control group or affiliated service group issue exists are beyond the scope of this book, but if you answered yes to any of these questions you should seek advice from an expert. Even if you don't answer yes to any of these questions, a competent advisor should ask you these questions early in the process.

The Six Core Elements of a Successful Retirement Plan

Once the decision has been made to implement a retirement plan, core elements of a successful plan need to be evaluated and implemented. There are six core elements of a successful plan, and each section of this text will explore each one of them.

1. Plan Design
   The first step in implementing a company sponsored retirement plan is to decide which type of plan is best for your business based on a number of factors such as company form and function, employee demographics, expected participation, goals of the owners and executives, etc. A good plan design will drive the purpose of the plan towards the objectives envisioned by the company.

2. Fiduciary Controls
   Proper fiduciary controls are one of the most critical aspects of a successful retirement plan. With good fiduciary controls in place, the plan will run smoothly and keep responsible parties

---

8   Simoneaux, Sarah. *Retirement Plan Consulting for Financial Professionals, 4th Edition.* Arlington: ASPPA, 2012. Print.

in good graces with the regulating agencies and the plan participants. Failing to understand your fiduciary roles and responsibilities can spell disaster for the responsible parties and the retirement plan.

3. Service Provider Selection and Retention
   Companies sponsoring retirement plans will need help running their plans, and for that they will turn to service providers. It's essential to understand the different roles and responsibilities each service provider plays, and good processes will ensure necessary services are provided while maintaining reasonable contracts and expenses.

4. Investment Management
   Proper management of plan investments ensures that the investments are appropriate, perform adequately against their benchmarks, and in the end help drive plan performance. Investment management is a key function in overall plan health, and for this many plan sponsors will seek outside assistance from experts with the skills and technology to guide their investment strategies.

5. Administrative Management
   Managing the day-to-day aspects of the plan is a function where typically some of the responsibility is retained in house. Administrative management can be complex, and many potential plan sponsors shy away from offering retirement plans due to the perceived burdens administratively, but with a proper understanding of delegated roles and responsibilities, administrative tasks can be easily managed.

6. Plan Health and Performance

Often overlooked, the vision of the plan can evolve into great success by evaluating performance metrics and driving desired outcomes. When plan sponsors aren't setting goals and objectives for the plan regularly, the plan may stagnate and lower the perceived value of the benefit by the employees and prospective recruits. Additionally, driving plan performance will help rank and file employees save for retirement while allowing owners and highly compensated employees to contribute more to their own accounts.

Summary

In this section we learned how important retirement planning is for American workers today, and how a corporate sponsored retirement plan can play an integral role in that regard. The shift away from pension plans and the minimal role social security will play in the future leaves the responsibility for planning and preparation on the worker, who is typically ill prepared to set forth and implement a formal plan without professional advice. Employers can provide a substantial benefit for their employees by offering to help implement a retirement plan, and as we'll see in a later section there are many things employers can do to spur the initiative on behalf of their employees.

Ultimately the decision of whether to implement a retirement plan through the company will depend on several factors including the retirement planning needs of the owners and management, free cash flow consistency, other business interests of the owners, and acceptance by the corporate sponsor of the role and responsibility it will be required to play once the decision has been made to offer a retirement plan. As we will see in a later section, the responsibilities of the sponsoring employer should be clearly understood to get the plan off on the right foot from the start, or if you already have a plan in place, take the steps now to make sure the plan is managed consistently with your responsibilities.

A well run, properly managed retirement plan will have their officials paying attention to the areas of plan governance that have the greatest impact on the success or failure of the plan. A plan sponsor will have covered virtually all of their bases by utilizing good plan design, strong fiduciary controls, a process for vendor selection and retention, professional investment management, good administrative oversight, driving the health and performance of the plan. These critical areas I call the Six Core Elements of successful retirement plan management, and they should be the focal points of introspection for all retirement plan sponsors.

CORE ELEMENT 1:
PLAN DESIGN

THE STORY...

Several years ago a friend of mine asked me to help his brother, Terry, who owned a successful engineering firm. The business was growing with room for expansion, but the owner was frustrated because he was having problems recruiting talent and he believed, according to some recruits who passed on his employment offer for others, that it boiled down to a retirement plan that wasn't seen as competitive in the industry.

I met with the owner and discovered that the plan he offered was a SIMPLE IRA. A great starter plan and very easy to setup and administer, it is ideal for smaller businesses who don't have the resources to dedicate to a more complex plan design. Fortunately Terry's business had been very successful over the years but while his company grew, his benefits did not.

Digging a little deeper, I learned that many of the engineers on the payroll weren't even contributing to the plan (taking only the company's non-elective contributions). Terry allowed me to meet with the employees collectively, and I quickly discovered that although most of them felt like they needed something better and wanted someone to help them plan for retirement, few ever voiced their opinion beforehand. In doing nothing they were all doing something: choosing to ignore the issue rather than confront it.

After bringing in a local Third Party Administration firm (TPA), we determined that the conditions existed for Terry to construct a very competitive 401(k) and profit sharing plan. We suggested a plan that would encourage feedback from the existing employees, and using that feedback we were able to get the employees involved to a point where they felt genuinely vested in its development. In doing this I hoped that we would get the employees more involved in taking an active role in their futures.

We designed the plan to encourage maximum enrollment and increase participants' contributions up to a point where they would actually be making a serious impact on their retirement outcomes. We found service providers whose resources were compatible with feedback of the employees and as an additional free service we offered on site personalized financial consultation for any employee who wanted personalized advice.

In the end Terry had one of the most competitive retirement plans for his niche business, and that helped him attract the type of employees he needed to expand. Every single employee at the firm enrolled in the plan during the first enrollment period and the retirement plan in now a source of pride and prestige for the firm instead of an afterthought.

✱ ✱

Plan design is a critical component affecting the outcomes the sponsor desires. The best source of information on plan designs can be found with a competent advisor and third party administrator (TPA). For the purposes of our discussion, we're going to lightly touch on some of the basic types of plans, design issues, vendor considerations, and plan features. The goals of this section are to:

✓ Introduce you to basic plan designs and features;
✓ Learn about safe harbor plans and how they affect owner deferrals;
✓ Review the difference between participant and trustee directed accounts;
✓ Discuss various types of arrangements with vendors.

TRAP #3

CHOOSING THE WRONG PLAN DESIGN

Choosing the wrong plan design from the outset can fail to produce the desired goals and objectives that the employer is seeking. This initial but critical step is the first failure we commonly see with retirement plans, and employers need to continually re-evaluate whether the current plan design is promoting or hindering the objectives of the company, the plan and its participants.

Types of Plans

When deciding to offer a plan, the first step is to consider what you what to accomplish (see "Questions to Ask Yourself Prior to Sponsoring a Plan" in the previous section). Next, we start to look at different plan design options.

The details of these different plan options are covered enough to warrant only a cursory review because this is really a question that you should consult with an advisor and TPA about before proceeding. But I'll go over some basics to give you an idea of what you may be looking at, but it will not be a comprehensive analysis of the different rules and regulations pertaining to each option.

Defined Benefit Plans

Defined benefit plans are the "pension" plans, providing lifetime income payments and sometimes survivor benefits. The rules are very complex and will not be discussed in any significant detail here. The premise behind a defined benefit plan is to provide a certain benefit, or income stream, to the employee at retirement. These plans generally favor older employers with younger employees.

Employer contributions are mandatory; after tax employee contributions may be allowed but are rarely utilized.[9] The benefit is usually based on years of service, compensation, or some combination. The employer, by way of a trustee, has total control over the investment of the plan assets and thus the employee plays no role in investment decision making processes. Social security benefits can sometimes be integrated with the calculation to offset some benefit. The IRC prescribes the maximum benefit allowed; in 2014 the maximum annual benefit a beneficiary can receive is $210,000.

Certain defined benefit plans are required to be insured by the Pension Benefit Guarantee Corporation (PBGC), a government agency created to protect employee pension benefits. As such, those plans required to be covered must pay a premium to the PBGC and also must report to the PBGC if certain events take place that may indicate problems with the plan.

Due to the amount of actuarial work required, these plans can be expensive to administer. Likewise, inaccurate actuarial assumptions caused several large, underfunded pension plans to be taken over by the PBGC, which helped to spur Congress to pass the Pension Protection Act (PPA) in 2006. Among many other things, the PPA set standards and metrics for actuarial assumptions that apply across the board. Defined benefit plans have mostly fallen out of favor because of their complexity, cost, and liability on the sponsor to provide the promised benefits, but still may be a viable benefit if the demographics are advantageous and it is structured properly.

Defined Contribution Plans

Defined contribution plans are retirement plans that are established with the focus on contributions, not benefits. Defined contribution plans are funded from employee savings, employer contributions, or both. In most defined contribution plans, the majority of savings will

---

9   Simoneaux, S. (2012). *Retirement Plan Consulting for Financial Professionals, 4th Edition.* Arlington: ASPPA.

come from the employee. The following sections will detail the variety of defined contribution plans available.

Profit Sharing Plans

Profit sharing plans are plans set up by an employer to provide a deductible contribution to employees of up to 25% of their compensation, with the latter benefiting from tax deferral. Employees usually do not make contributions to profit sharing plans, and may or may not direct the investments in their accounts. Profit sharing plans must use a predetermined formula for distribution among the eligible participants, prescribed by the Internal Revenue Code (IRC). Despite the name, a company need not have profits in any given year to pay out the profit share. The employer retains the discretion as to whether to contribute to the plan and how much.

Profit sharing plans have several design option, each one increasing in complexity and administrative cost, but also may provide for better contributions arrangements for owners and management. In order of complexity from least to most are pro-rata formulas, integrated, age-weighted and cross-tested:

- *Pro-Rata Formula*: the contribution is allocated as a percentage of eligible compensation only.

  For example, if the contribution is ten percent of compensation, an employee with $100,000 in compensation would receive a maximum $10,000 contribution to his profit sharing plan, whereas an employee with $10,000 in compensation would receive a maximum $1,000 contribution.

- *Integrated with Social Security:* this plan permits contributions above the taxable wage base (the maximum amount of earned income which social security taxes are paid), allowing participants with earned income above the taxable wage base to receive a larger percentage of contributions.

- *Age-Weighted:* this type of plan determines calculations based on compensation and age where older participants will receive a larger contribution than younger participants with the equivalent compensation.

- *Cross-Tested or New Comparability:* this arrangement allows contributions based on employee "classifications". Employees are grouped into certain classes, and those classes are permitted to receive different percentages of contributions. This arrangement requires additional non-discrimination testing.

Most third party administrators are adept at working out the numbers based on a payroll census and coming up with the best arrangement to meet the needs and goals of the company. Profit sharing plans are frequently used in conjunction with 401(k) plans. The IRS limits profit sharing contributions, (technically all qualified plan contributions) by way of the annual addition limits. In 2014, the most you can contribute to all qualified accounts combined is $52,000 per year (there are some exceptions for certain "hybrid plans" discussed later).

Simplified Employee Pensions/SIMPLE IRAs/SIMPLE 401(k)'s

Simplified Employee Pensions (SEP), SIMPLE IRAs, and SIMPLE 401(k)'s are three basic plan designs that can be started with minimal cost and administration.

Simplified Employee Pension (SEP)

Flexibility is the greatest with the simplified employee pension (SEP). In this arrangement, contributions are determined by the employer. She can contribute one year, not the next, and so on. With a SEP, no employee contributions are permitted, and contributions are immediately vested to the participant.

A SEP functions similar to a profit sharing arrangement, because contributions as a percentage of income must be the same for all eligible employees, but no more than 25% of compensation for each participant. SEPs are also more liberal in terms of which employees may be eligible to participate than the other two arrangements. SEPs will have to comply with a nondiscrimination test known as the "Top Heavy" test (nondiscrimination tests refer to contributions, eligibility is a separate consideration).

SIMPLE IRA

A simple IRA is an arrangement where the employee can contribute up to a certain percent of pay (currently three percent), and the employer matches. If the employee does not contribute, the employer still must match two percent of the employee's compensation. Contributions are immediately vested, and participants direct their own investments similar to an Individual Retirement Account.

These plans are less flexible than a SEP, but they are better suited for smaller companies that cannot accept the administrative duties and costs associated with more complex plan designs. Simple IRAs have distribution penalties for the first two years for participants. There are currently no nondiscrimination tests for contributions. Simple IRAs are not available for employers with more than 100 employees.

Simple 401(k)

Simple 401(k)'s are not common in the marketplace, but many of the rules are similar to the SIMPLE IRA. Employers make either a matching contribution of up to three percent of employee compensation, or a two percent non-elective contribution for all eligible employees. Contributions are likewise vested immediately.

Simple 401(k) plan sponsors are not permitted to offer any other type of retirement plan concurrently. The biggest differences are in eligibility and distributions: more employees may be eligible, and distributions are less restrictive than SIMPLE IRAs including the option for loans if the plan sponsor permits. Simple 401(k)'s do not have the restrictive non-discrimination rules associated with traditional 401(k) plans.

Money Purchase Plans (MPP)

Money purchase plans (MPP) are similar in structure to a defined benefit plan, but nevertheless are considered defined contribution. MPPs allow a deductible contribution of up to 25% of employee compensation, but that contribution is fixed at inception and mandatory unless the plan is amended. Additionally, the MPP is subject to the same rules for timing of deposits as defined benefit plans (not covered in this edition).

As a result of the inflexibility and funding requirements, these plans are rarely found in the market today because of changes to the rules for profit sharing plans making them more attractive. They are similar to pensions in that there is a mandatory annuity option for participants, allowing for income benefits over a lifetime.

The Traditional 401(k) Plan

The name, 401(k), comes from the subsection in Internal Revenue Code which allowed these plans in the first place. Specifically, the 401(k) provides for pre-tax income deferral via payroll withholdings, deposited into a trust or insurance separate account which has the added benefit of being tax deferred. The employer may or may not match the employee's contributions, but 401(k)'s are subject to nondiscrimination testing for contributions. Because of this, they carry a significant administrative burden and many of the moving parts in a 401(k) are outsourced to other vendors or "service providers".

The participant's 401(k) account is treated very similar to IRAs for tax purposes, but there are some notable differences. 401(k)'s allow much greater annual deferrals than IRAs, up to $17,500 per in year in 2014, $23,000 per year if you are over the age of 50.[10] Participation in a 401(k) as an employee precludes the participant from required minimum distributions at age 70½, unlike individual IRAs. Loans can also be made by the participant, at the employer's discretion, unlike IRAs.

Like other qualified plans, 401(k)'s are subject to eligibility and vesting rules although vesting options in a 401(k) can be structured to a restrictive schedule, which is especially important in high turnover industries.

Safe Harbor 401(k) Plan

Safe harbor 401(k) plans are an option for sponsors who want to maximize their contributions when rank and file participation in the plan may be low, or other demographics exist that would normally limit contributions from highly compensated employees. Safe harbor plans eliminate some of the nondiscrimination testing for employee contributions if constructed properly.

Safe harbor plans require matching contributions of the first four, five, or six percent of compensation depending on what the plan sponsors elect, or a non-elective contribution of three percent to all eligible employees. Safe harbor contributions are immediately vested to participants and require certain disclosure be made regarding the intention to qualify for the safe harbor.

Solo 401(k) Plans

You can start a 401(k) for only yourself if you are a business owner with no employees, but there are different rules for individual or solo 401(k)'s. Consult an advisor or third party administrator if you have questions about them.

---

10   Internal Revenue Service. (2014, Oct). *Retirement Topics - Contributions.* Retrieved from IRS: www.irs.gov/Retirement-Plans/Plan-Participant,-Employee/Retirement-Topics-Contributions

ESOP/KSOP

Employee Stock Ownership Plans (ESOPs) are plans that invest primarily in the securities of the underlying business. This allows participation by the employees in corporate ownership. ESOPs are primarily used in the process of transferring ownership of the company to employees because owners are retiring. Because of their nature investing in securities with limited marketability, ESOPs are highly regulated with special rules. A KSOP is an ESOP with a 401(k). ESOPs/KSOPs will not be covered in any further detail in this edition.

Multiemployer Plans and Multiple Employer Plans (MEPs)

Although they sound the same, these are two distinctive entities. Multiemployer plans are plans in which more than one contributing employer participates and whose terms are created by one or more collective bargaining agreements between one or more unions and employers.

Multiple Employer Plans (or MEPs) consist of all other plans with more than one employer participating. MEPs usually have participating employers who have some commonality between them (associations, trade groups, et cetera), but "open" MEPs which are structured when participating employers are distinctly different, are growing in popularity for a variety of reasons.

MEPs and multiemployer plans are plans that harbor many different design characteristics already mentioned, such as 401(k), Roth 401(k), profit sharing, etc. Each plan is designed uniquely based on the collective bargaining agreement for multiemployer plans or by the direction of the adopting plan sponsor in the case of a MEP.

MEPs have been growing in popularity recently. One of the most attractive benefits of a MEP is that the adopting MEP sponsor, usually by committee, assumes a significant portion of the fiduciary duties or appoints professionals to assume those fiduciary duties, relieving the participating employer of a significant portion of those duties. However, MEPs have some very specific considerations that should be carefully analyzed before opting to participate in one.

Hybrid Plans

Hybrid plans are plans that generally fit somewhere between a defined contribution and defined benefit plan, with some elements of both.

Target Benefit Plans

Target benefit plans were originally conceived as a hybrid plan, with elements of both defined contribution and defined benefit plans. Similar to MPPs with fixed contribution schedules, these plans were designed to allow higher contributions for older, higher compensated workers. Target benefit plans have certain limitations that make them uncompetitive with other options now available, and are seldom found in the market.

Cash Balance Plans

Although technically considered a defined benefit plan, cash balance plans function in practice more like a hybrid plan and are often used in conjunction with a 401(k) and profit sharing plan. Cash balance plans can provide significant savings opportunities for plan with the right demographics, e.g. employers with older owners and highly compensated employees, and a younger and less compensated workforce. Cash balance plans are often used in conjunction with 401(k) and profit sharing plans because integrating all three plans together can maximize the effectiveness of the cash balance plan.

In some cases, older owners can contribute $200,000 to almost $300,000 per year (including the maximum contributions to a 401(k) and profit sharing), deferring taxes on that income resulting in significant tax savings and significant accumulation. The Pension

Protection Act of 2006 relaxed some of the rules related to cash balance plans and the IRS just recently issued some long awaited guidance on them, and as such they are rapidly gaining in popularity for businesses that have the demographics that allow them to take advantage of the cash balance plan's significant benefits.

Cash balance plans offer owners and highly compensated employees the opportunity to squeeze significant tax favored contributions into a small time frame. Candidates are usually looking to maximize deferrals for owners and key employees while savings significantly on taxable income. Cash balance plans have "targeted" investment returns, and typically the returns are targeted at rates lower than equity investment returns.

Volatility in the investment returns can create contribution problems for cash balance plan sponsors. Candidates need to understand that contribution requirements may increase or decrease depending on the actual rate of return of the investments. Cash balance plans are portable to the employees when severed from employment, but employees generally do not have control over the investments in the plan. Like other qualified plans, balances are protected from claims of creditors.[11]

The Power of Proper Plan Design

The power of proper plan design helps to offset one of the biggest challenges for highly compensated earners: the limitations on the amount of contributions in a retirement plan. The annual contribution limits for defined contribution plans are as follows (2014):

Traditional IRA	$5,500	OR	$6,500 (50 y/o or older)
SEP	25% of pay	OR	$52,000 (Lesser of)
SIMPLE IRA	$12,500	OR	$15,000 (50 y/o or older)
401(k) Only	$17,500	OR	$23,000 (50 y/o or older)
401(k) + Profit Sharing	$52,000	OR	$57,500 (50 y/o or older)

---

11 Kravitz, D., Guidroz, K., & Sansone, S. (2010). *Beyond the 401(k)*. Encino: Kravitz Publishing.

This demonstrates a type of "reverse discrimination" against highly compensated employees who may need to save significantly more than the average worker to maintain their lifestyle in retirement. However, the Pension Protection Act of 2006 is widely considered to be "business owner friendly" legislation that permits more creative plan design features. This can be very attractive for business owners or professionals who fall into one or more of these categories:

• Needs to save more annually than the traditional dollar limits;

• Wants to contribute a higher percentage of compensation than the 25% limit;

• Needs to squeeze twenty years of savings into ten or less;

• Wants to maximize the benefits for owners and/or key management;

• Professional service organizations, such a law firms, medical and accounting practices;

• Highly profitable companies;

• Companies with older owners/key personnel and younger rank and file employees;

Business owners typically have two main objectives: maximize benefits for the owners and minimize the costs. This is where proper plan design can come into play. With the right plan design we can sometimes get contributions as high as **seven times the defined contribution annual limits with as much as 98% of the outlay going for the benefit of the owners and/or key personnel**. These designs usually incorporate 401(k)'s with advanced "gateway" profit sharing designs combined with some type of defined benefit, hybrid, or medical reimbursement plan.

Many employers welcome the cost and challenges associated with running a retirement plan for the employees that utilize the benefit but often find themselves discouraged when they are forced, due to discrimination rules, to reward employees who don't "help themselves," or employees who are in high turnover positions. Proper plan design can often mitigate these concerns by re-structuring how and to whom discretionary profit sharing contributions can be given, thereby getting more of those discretionary contributions into the hands of the people who are most important to the company.

In addition to maximizing benefits and minimizing costs, under the right circumstances and with a good plan design, a business owner can structure a retirement plan as part of a business succession plan, allowing them to extract the value of the business in cash, over time, while still maintaining control and incentivizing their employees by making them stakeholders in the success of the business.

The power of proper plan design can best be observed in analyzing some quick numbers. We'll look at a couple brief examples:

A special thanks to Sandra Turner, President of Retirement Plan Specialists, for assisting with the following example sections.

Self-Employed Example

John is a 55 year old self employed consultant making a schedule C net profit of $250,000 this year. John has nothing saved for retirement, but wants to save as much as possible over the next ten years. His tax situation looks roughly as follows:

Net Profit	$250,000
Total Deductions (1/2 SE)	-$10,695
Qualified Plan Deductions	-0-
Adjusted Gross Income	$239,305
Less Itemized Deductions	-$15,000
Taxable Income	$224,305
Taxes Owed	$74,021
Total Tax Owed (Plus SE Tax)	$95,410

Based on his particular situation, we examined four possibilities at maximum contributions: a Simplified Employee Pension, a Solo 401(k), a Cash Balance plan, and a combination 401(k)/CB plan. Here's how these plans can reduce his taxes:

	SEP	401(k)	CB	401(k)+CB
Taxable Income	$176,444	$165,305	$104,653	$77,168
Taxes Owed	$58,227	$54,551	$34,535	$25,465
Total Tax Owed (Plus SE Tax)	$79,616	$75,940	$55,925	$46,855
Total Tax Savings	$15,794	$19,470	$39,485	$48,555

John is able to reduce his total tax liability by as much as 48%! John would be eligible to make larger contributions over time, but we'll assume his contribution levels, income, and tax rates remain constant for the next ten years. Assuming a five percent annual rate of return on his savings:

	SEP	401(k)	CB	401(k)+CB
Annual Disposable Income	$122,523	$115,060	$74,423	$56,008
Amount to Savings	$47,861	$59,000	$119,653	$147,138
Future Value of Savings over 10 years	$601,991	$742,096	$1,504,978	$1,850,682

Single Owner, Professional Service Company Example

Sarah is a 60 year old successful attorney with a small, highly specialized legal practice. She has four employees. Her employees' gross salaries are within $30,000-$50,000 per year, with Sarah's salary at $260,000. Sarah has a 401(k) safe harbor plan in which she makes a dollar for dollar up to four percent of salary with a discretionary non-elective contribution so that all employees get a contribution that is equal to the same percentage to their pay. Under this specific plan design, approximately __75%__ of Sarah's outlay for contributions to the plan go for her benefit, with the remaining 25% to her employees.

Having only been saving about $50,000 a year, Sarah realized she needed to save at least another $1,000,000 to maintain her lifestyle in the remaining five to ten years she would be practicing, so we explored other plan design options for her. When we examined a cash balance plan using the 401(k) safe harbor with a three percent match using new comparability rules, we were able to boost Sarah's benefit up to almost __95%__ of her outlay and squeeze more than $200,000 per year into her retirement plan for at least the next five years. Sarah's tax liability also dropped dramatically.

Participant Directed Accounts vs. Trustee Directed Accounts

Investments in a retirement plan are invested to grow for the benefit of the participants, but who actually makes the decisions about what investments to use? The answer is: it depends. One thing for certain is that the sponsoring employer will almost always have some say in what options are used or available.

Generally speaking, the plan sponsor will decide in which accounts participants may choose their own investments, but in some cases participant self-direction is the only option available, such as in SIMPLE IRA and SEP plans. A participant directed account is an investment account in which the participant makes some or all of the investment decisions. The extent to which the participant can control the investments depends on the type of plan and the nature of the arrangement.

In cases like the SEP and SIMPLE IRA where the plan sponsor selects the vendor but otherwise plays no role in the investment process, the participant's choices for investment options are limited only by what the vendor allows the participant to use. For instance, a mutual fund company offering a SEP plan may offer a line-up of funds from a pre-selected menu. In other cases such as plans offered directly from a brokerage company, the investments allowed in the plan may only be limited by what the plan is legally allowed to contain (e.g. no collectibles, coins, certain speculative derivatives, real estate, life insurance, etc.) but otherwise open to a broad universe of available investments such as mutual funds, ETFs, individual stocks and bonds, etc.

There are also some types of plans never allowed for participant direction of the investments. Examples are defined benefit or "pension" plans and cash balance plans (technically the IRS has not issued any guidance on participant direction in cash balance plans, but it is not generally recommended at this time). These plans are usually pooled accounts, managed by a trustee (also known as trustee directed). In this case, participant's assets are pooled together in a trust and the trustee, usually a competent investment manager or committee, will make investments collectively for the benefit of all the participants. The trustee(s) will generally have complete control over what investments are used and when to buy or sell, unless limited by the language in the trust documents.

For accounts that permit either participant or trustee investment direction, the plan sponsor first must choose whether to allow participant direction at all. If there are multiple plans combined such as a profit sharing and a 401(k), the sponsor must decide how each account will be handled. In most cases where participant direction is allowed, a "responsible fiduciary" will help create a line-up of investment options for the plan. Participants will then choose to allocate their assets among the investments in that line-up.

Deciding on participant or trustee investment direction is a very important step in the plan design process, and each has its own unique advantages and disadvantages. Retaining control of the investments using a trustee model can reduce administrative burdens and save time and expense, but can also increase liability unless you follow proper processes (see Core Element 2 "Fiduciary Controls") and outsource some liability by retaining competent service providers (see Core Element 3 "Service Provider Retention"). Some studies suggest that trustee directed accounts consistently outperform participant directed accounts, due mostly to professional money management that avoids emotional investment mistakes.

Alternatively, many plan sponsors believe that allowing participants to direct their own investments will relieve them of any liability with regards to the investments. As we will see in Core Element 4 "Investment Management", this is often not the case. Plan sponsors may retain liability for the investments made available to the participants, and unbelievably even for the participants' own investment decisions, whether they actively make those decisions or not! However, there are ways to outsource and reduce this liability. We will see later what steps should be taken to minimize liabilities associated with participant directed accounts.

TRAP #4

NOT UNDERSTANDING
THE INVESTMENT PLATFORM

Failing to understand the types of investment platforms available and not choosing the best platform for the needs of the plan and participants can lead to confusion, especially when plan participants try and compare the investment options under the plan with commonly available data from similar funds that do not correspond to their actual investment options.

Investment Platforms

Investment platforms serve as the engine behind retirement plans, and as such it's important to be able to identify the different types. Investment platforms are closely associated with the record keeper. Record keepers will be discussed in more detail soon, but generally they are responsible for tracking transactions, including contributions and participant directed investment allocations. As such, they are usually the face of the plan for the participant. Ease of interaction, technology, accessibility and interface will often be the first impressions to the participant and therefore it's important to ensure this results in a pleasant experience for them by choosing the right one.

Record keepers serve as the largest identifiable sales force in the retirement plan world, but for many companies record keeping is more of a cost center rather than a source of revenue. Investment platforms (and their associated record keeping services) generally come in two distinct flavors: insurance separate account platforms and Net Asset Value (NAV) platforms, and there are several variations of NAV platforms. Insurance and NAV are segregated mainly because the "separate accounts" associated with insurance companies are distinctly different from most other accounts which are NAV.

NAV platforms include brokerage, mutual fund, and independent vendors. Note that many of these arrangements can offer bundled product solutions utilizing multiple services such as record keeping, third party administration, investment management, etc. More on the details of these kinds of service providers can be found in the Prelude to Core Element 3 "The Roles of Service Providers".

Insurance Platforms

Insurance platforms are offered by insurance companies. While invested, the assets of the plan are usually held in vehicles known as "separate accounts" as opposed to trusts (although there are some insurance companies who offer investment platforms utilizing trusts and hence look like NAV platforms). Platforms that utilize separate accounts are typically referred to as group annuities.

Group annuities are insurance platforms that also provide the participant the option to convert the account's assets into an annuity providing lifetime income if they so choose. The separate accounts of group annuities are pooled investments in which participants purchase "units". Profits and losses in the separate accounts are distributed evenly based on the number of units owned.

Insurance related platforms using separate accounts will have a menu of investment options available for the plan; a separate discretionary investment manager or in house investment committee would have the responsibility for choosing the core menu available to participants. Typically the investment windows will consist of proprietary funds, "sub-advised" funds ("sub-advised" funds are managed by entities that don't actually have custody the assets) and usually non-proprietary funds. Sub-Advised funds may look and sound like their true mutual fund cousins but are not the same and do not have CUSIP numbers that allow tracking and valuation on the open market (CUSIPs are simply a standardized tracking number for U.S. based securities).

Note that "separate accounts" are not the same as "separately managed accounts" or SMAs, which refer to portfolios of assets under the management of a professional investment firm known a Registered Investment Advisor (RIA). These accounts will be discussed in Core Element 4 "Investment Management".

Net Asset Value (NAV) Platforms

Net Asset Value (NAV) platforms are offered by banks and broker-dealers, mutual fund providers, independent providers, and some insurance companies. NAV platforms allow participants to track and compare performance of their funds with the corresponding security's CUSIP, providing for better tracking and transparency than separate accounts. Although the term "NAV" is most commonly associated with mutual funds, in the context of retirement investment platforms it is usually referred to as any account platform that is not an insurance separate account.

NAV platforms are most commonly associated with traditional individual brokerage accounts or individual retirement accounts held at a bank or broker-dealer, and the NAV pricing model is something that anyone with an account at one of these financial institutions will be somewhat familiar with even if they didn't know what it was called. The three main types of NAV platforms are mutual fund and insurance platforms, brokerage platforms, and independent record-keeping platforms.

NAV Mutual Fund and NAV Insurance Platforms

Mutual fund platforms are NAV platforms associated with a particular fund family. They are found in the retail mutual fund industry that offer SEP and SIMPLE IRA types of plans, and there are a few that can manage 401(k)'s and other similar plan designs.

Insurance platforms are NAV versions of group annuities that do not utilize separate accounts. The insurance companies that offer these platforms generally require a minimum asset level or other requirements to contract with them.

Mutual fund and insurance companies usually offer custodial and/or recordkeeping functions as part of the platform (see the "Prelude for Core Element 3"). A mutual fund or insurance firm may require the plan sponsor or trustee to either select the fund lineup from a predetermined list or require a certain number of proprietary funds on the window. This is because recordkeeping services are expensive, and costs are reimbursed through pre-determined fee sharing arrangements with funds on the list or by the use of proprietary funds themselves (more on this in a later section). Some fund or insurance companies will allow an "open architecture" window for larger plans.

Any platform that requires the use of proprietary or predetermined funds demand a different level of due diligence on the part of the fiduciary who has the responsibility to contract with that service provider (see Core Element 3 on "Service Provider Retention").

Brokerage Platforms

Brokerage platforms are NAV platforms that are usually associated with trustee directed plans and a special participant directed investment window called a Self-Directed Brokerage Account (refer to Core Element 4 "Investment Management"). Brokerage platforms are typically used with a bank or broker-dealer custodian. Brokerage platforms are more of an "open window" to the investment universe, limited usually only by the custodians approved list of investments, which is usually quite expansive, offering great flexibility and options.

Brokerage platforms can also have custodians other than a bank or broker-dealer, as in a trust. These platforms may allow investments in types of securities that are otherwise unavailable under traditional custodians. Although this arrangement may be permissible for trustee directed accounts with expert investment management, it can present unique challenges and concerns for both trustee and especially participant directed accounts.

Independent Recordkeeping Platforms

Independent platforms are NAV recordkeeping platforms that have no affiliation with insurance or investments. In this sense, they are completely independent. They are almost always "open architecture", allowing most mutual funds and other options that are available on the open market through the National Securities Clearing Corporation (NSCC), but most will use an expansive list of approved securities. Independent platform fees may seem more expensive for recordkeeping, but often they are just more transparent.

Summary

Plan design is the first essential core element to a successful plan. Poor plan design can result in undesired outcomes and a benefit that is not competitive. Prospective employees increasingly understand the value of this benefit, and good plan design can improve the recruitment and retention of key talent.

Understanding the benefits, drawbacks and risks associated with each plan design is a starting point for employers who intend to offer these benefits. While advisors and other service providers can substantially assist a business in determining what plan design is appropriate to them, a fundamental understanding of plan design basics before engaging in more in depth analysis can reduce time spent in entertaining design options that are not in line with the goals of the business.

A significant step in the process is determining to what extent, if any, participants have control over investing their contributions. Whether retaining trustee direction over investments or allowing participants to make their own decisions, each option carries its own unique risk/reward characteristics that plan sponsors need to be aware of. And when participant direction is elected, a variety of investment platforms exist for various plan designs, each with their own set of benefits and drawbacks.

CORE ELEMENT 2: FIDUCIARY CONTROLS

If you read only a single part of this book, it needs to be this section. Most closely-held business owners are busy keeping their business afloat and people employed, and consequentially the retirement plan is #247 out of 500 things that you need to do today and hence not on your radar. This section is the heart of the book and the reason why I wrote it.

In my experience 80-90% of the plan sponsors I meet with have heard the terms in this section before but have just a smattering of understanding with regards to what it means to them. What I would hope you understand when you finish this section is that:

- *You have a duty to fulfill;*
- *There are REAL and PERSONAL consequences for breaching that duty in terms of both time and expense;*
- *And there is a plethora of help available if you only seek it.*

* *

The single most important concept for a sponsor of a retirement plan is to understand who the fiduciaries are and what their roles and responsibilities are. Failing as a fiduciary is the primary cause of action for enforcement, litigation, and liability. The goals of this section are to:

✓ Define "fiduciary" and provide some background;

✓ Understand what plans fall under the fiduciary responsibility rules;

✓ Explain different types of decisions you will need to make;

✓ Define the standards of care you are legally bound to;

✓ Show who can hold you accountable to those standards;

✓ Demonstrate best practices to implement in your business to protect yourself.

TRAP #5

NOT KNOWING WHAT AN ERISA FIDUCIARY IS AND IS NOT

Understanding your roles and responsibilities with respect to your retirement plan are critical because it is what the LAW demands of you and what the regulators EXPECT of you. Failing here is never excusable, and it can cost you both legally and personally.

The Confusion

The concept of fiduciary responsibility is at the heart of retirement plan law, and is the single most important concept to understand for any retirement plan sponsor, but herein lies the crux of the problem in the industry: plan sponsors may know the meaning of the word fiduciary, but few understand the context to ERISA and *fewer* understand the responsibilities or the gravity that those duties imply. So before we begin to discuss who is and who isn't a fiduciary we have to begin by defining fiduciary, especially as it relates to ERISA.

The Common Law Fiduciary Defined

The "fiduciary" is a person(s) who is responsible for decision making, and also the one to have their feet held to the fire when something goes wrong. The Merriam-Webster definition of a fiduciary is "a person in a position of authority whom the law obligates to act solely on behalf of the person he or she represents…fiduciaries may not seek personal benefit from their transactions with those they represent."[12] In general, a fiduciary is a person of trust acting in the capacity for someone or something else, and handles that responsibility with the highest duty of care and loyalty.

The definition of fiduciary in this context is the result of trust law, the Uniform Prudent Investors Act (UPIA),[13] and relevant regulating agency definitions (Securities and Exchange Commission and state law in particular). ERISA fiduciaries are defined differently, although the heart of the responsibility is very similar. It is important to be able to distinguish a common law fiduciary from an ERISA fiduciary because ERISA fiduciaries are held to very specific legal standards that are significantly more precise than common law fiduciaries.

Plans Covered By ERISA Fiduciary Rules

ERISA §401 defines what types of plans are covered under ERISA fiduciary rules in the broader section of the legislation. In general, every employee benefit plan is covered EXCEPT:

- Unfunded plans providing deferred compensation to select groups of employees or executives;

- Certain agreements that provide retirement benefits to a retired or deceased business partner or their beneficiaries.

---

12 "Fiduciary." *Merriam-Webster.com*. Merriam-Webster, 2014. Web. 11 May 2014.

13 Uniform Law Commission. (n.d.). *Prudent Investor Act Summary*. Retrieved from Uniform Law Commission: www.uniformlaws.org/ActSummary. aspx?title=Prudent%20Investor%20Act

Exempt are the aforementioned "non-qualified" benefit arrangements (see the Introduction) and eligible earn-outs, buy-sell arrangements, and similar constructs that fall within the exemptions. Aside from these exceptions, every other employee benefit plan is obligated by law to act in accordance to the rules prescribed for fiduciaries in the remainder of that legislation.

Holding You Accountable: The Regulating Agencies

Retirement plans are regulated by three agencies of the federal government: The Department of Labor (DOL), The Department of Treasury (specifically the IRS), and the Pension Benefit Guarantee Corporation (PBGC). Of these, the most important to the employer are the DOL and the IRS. The Employee Benefit Security Administration (EBSA) is the agency within the Department of Labor tasked with the enforcement of all pension and welfare benefit plans, including the Affordable Care Act.

From an operational perspective, the two primary areas of concern for the employer are tax compliance and legal compliance. The IRS enforces the plan's compliance with tax rules per the Internal Revenue Code (IRC), including operational and reporting compliance. The DOL/EBSA enforces legal compliance under ERISA and the fiduciary operations of the plan. Both of these agencies can audit any plan covered under their jurisdiction. Although these agencies generally investigate different areas of plan governance, they *can and will* communicate with each other if they uncover a failure deserving the attention of the other agency.

The ERISA Fiduciary

ERISA Section 3(21)(A) defines a fiduciary to be a person(s) who:

i. Exercises any discretionary authority or discretionary control over plan management or any authority or control over the disposition of assets;

ii. Renders investment advice for a fee or compensation, direct or indirect, with respect to money or property of the plan, or who has the authority or responsibility to do so;

iii. Exercises any discretionary authority or discretionary responsibility in administration of such plan.

The important take away is that anyone with control or discretion with respect to plan management, assets, or administration is an ERISA fiduciary. Also, anyone who renders *investment advice* for a fee or compensation is also a fiduciary. In any given retirement plan, there is at least one person or entity listed in the plan document as the named fiduciary. Being named by the plan documents, this person(s) has expressly defined control and discretion over the plan, and consequently may have the most significant liability.

Typically, the plan's named fiduciary will appoint a "plan administrator" who is generally responsible for plan administration, and a "trustee" who will be responsible for assets held in trust. In many plan adoption agreements, the named fiduciary is the same as the plan administrator. But understand there are practically unlimited ways of dividing responsibilities, depending on each individual plan's arrangements. Other types of fiduciaries are covered under the "Appointed Fiduciaries" section.

A specific distinction should be made at this time between "plan sponsor" and the "plan administrator", found on the "IRS Form 5500" and distinguished in greater detail in the next section. The distinction was recently cleared up by a Supreme Court decision. The Supreme Court on February 19th, 2011 found that a plan sponsor (the employer most commonly) acts in a "settlor" capacity by creating the plan's terms and conditions, executing a document describing those terms and conditions, and providing a procedure for making amendments. The plan administrator acts in a "fiduciary" capacity by managing the plan according to the plan documents and providing disclosures to participants and beneficiaries. Although they can and often are the same entity, their roles are distinct from each other which can lead to a situation where decisions are made by the same person(s) wearing "different hats"; this often serves as a backdrop for confusion, misunderstandings and mistakes.

Typically fiduciaries are named in the plan documents; *however courts have found that a person(s) can be determined to be fiduciary by consequence of their express, functional, or de facto control or management whether or not they are named in the plan document as a fiduciary.*[14]

This is a critical point to understand. One does not have to be named in any document as a fiduciary to be determined to be a fiduciary, nor does one have to acknowledge that status. There is a great deal of case law covering this area, and many times it's the unknowing, unwilling functional fiduciary that suddenly finds themselves liable for their own confusion.

The bottom line is that you can be held liable for any decisions or actions made you make whether or not you are named as a fiduciary in the plan document, if your actions or discretion fall under the definition of an ERISA fiduciary. One does not have to acknowledge or accept fiduciary status to be liable under ERISA.[15]

TRAP #6

IMPROPERLY DIFFERENTIATING BETWEEN NON-FIDUCIARY AND FIDUCIARY DECISIONS

Decisions made by plan officials fall under one of two categories: non-fiduciary and fiduciary decisions. Failing to understand which decisions fall under each category can lead to fiduciary failures which increase your liability and likely increase the costs to you due to corrective measures which may need to be taken, which you will be responsible for paying.

---

14   Jones, David and Ziga, Kathleen, and Chong, Sumi. *ERISA Fiduciary Responsibility and Liability.* Dechert LLP. PDF File.

15   St. Martin, Andree. *Fiduciary Issues in ERISA-Covered Plans.* Groom Law Group. 2005. PDF File.

Non-Fiduciary (Settlor) vs. Fiduciary Acts

Settlor acts are not governed by fiduciary laws. These would include, but not be limited to:

• Decisions to adopt, amend, or terminate a plan;

• Decisions regarding plan design and benefit structure;

• Determination of covered employees.

Settlor decisions are normally made by the entity associated with the title of "plan sponsor"; usually the employer. Settlor functions allows the employer to enjoy a great amount of discretion in the decision making process without concerns of violating ERISA.

There are some important caveats to understand. First, plan assets can never be used to pay for settlor activities; these costs must be paid by the plan sponsor.[16] For example, for a the decision to terminate a plan, any costs associated with researching that decision and the actual termination fees may not be paid for using plan assets. Another example would be costs associated with correcting plan errors; they must not be paid for using plan assets.

Second, the implementation of a settlor decision may involve fiduciary actions. An example would be an amendment to the plan document to offer loans to participants; although the decision to offer loans is a settlor decision, the operational decisions providing for the loans would be fiduciary in nature.

Third, there remain some interesting and unsettled discussions regarding certain types of decisions and whether they fall under the settlor or fiduciary category. These mostly concern features that can be argued as either plan design features or fiduciary permissible features.[17] You just need to know that there are matters that are not fully clarified,

---

16 Muir, Dana, and Stein, Norman. *Two Hats, One Head, No Heart: The Anatomy of the ERISA Settlor/Fiduciary Distinction*. 2013. PDF File.

17 Muir, Dana, and Stein, Norman. *Two Hats, One Head, No Heart: The Anatomy of the ERISA Settlor/Fiduciary Distinction*. 2013. PDF File.

and you should be careful in delineating between the two without guidance.

And finally, although the plan sponsor has leeway associated with plan design, benefits and coverage, you still must abide by the constraints of the Internal Revenue Code (IRC) and ERISA nondiscrimination, vesting, and other rules and regulations.

TRAP #7

FAILING TO UNDERSTAND THE DIVISION OF RESPONSIBILITY BETWEEN FIDUCIARIES

The differences between the allocations of responsibility between fiduciaries named in the plan documents and responsibilities delegated to other parties are frequently misunderstood and improperly executed. Even seemingly benign delegations of administrative responsibilities to in-house human resources personnel can lead to unintentional liability to both parties and improper oversight.

Allocating and Delegating Fiduciary Responsibilities

Most plans may permit a named fiduciary the power to allocate responsibility among other named fiduciaries that may manage and control certain aspects related to the plan, such as an investment manager, and an administrative manager, with the notable exception of trustee responsibilities. In addition to allocating responsibility among other named fiduciaries, responsibility may also be delegated to other, "unnamed" fiduciaries.

While ERISA restricts the ability to allocate responsibility only among named fiduciaries, the plan document usually provides the power of allocation and delegation. It's important that you understand the distinction if you are responsible for allocation and delegation.

Whereas allocation generally divides responsibilities is such a way as to indemnify a fiduciary against allocated responsibilities, delegated responsibilities do not provide such protection, and failures of delegation of responsibility can ultimately fall back on the fiduciary who made such delegations.[18]

Careful consideration should be given to determine whether the allocation or delegation is permissible per the plan documents, whether the appointee has the proper skill and resources to perform their requisite duties, and how the appointing fiduciary will monitor the appointee in the case of delegation. However, in certain circumstances fiduciaries can be held liable for the acts and/or omissions of the other fiduciaries, depending on the extent that the allocating/delegating fiduciary's actions contributed to the breach, what was known to and permitted by the delegating fiduciary, whether there was an effort to conceal a violation and what actions were taken once known. In any event, the delegating fiduciary always has a duty to monitor the delegated fiduciary and take action when necessary.

You will hear the term "co-fiduciary" mentioned by service providers or advisors, and although they are commonly used interchangeably they may have different meanings depending on the context. Often these services are marketed as an add-on to the services already offered by vendors. Co-fiduciaries in this context generally do not have clearly defined liability, outside of ERISA fiduciary duties outlined below, because they do not generally affect "control or management" of the plan's assets, management or administration but merely provide advice or guidance.

The determination of co-fiduciary liability is a facts and circumstances consideration; although they may not have explicit control or discretion, they could be found to have de facto control given the circumstances which would open up the exposure of liability. Though they can be useful, they do not necessarily absolve the appointing

---

18   Baker, Jason, and Abbey, David. "A Fiduciary by Any Other Name…Thoughts on Properly Delegating Fiduciary Duties." *Benefits Law Journal, Vol. 22, No. 1.* 2009. PDF File.

fiduciary responsibility over the decisions made since a co-fiduciary with no discretion or control has no power to affect those decisions.

Special consideration needs to be given regarding the appointment and delegation of trustees. The named fiduciary can appoint a trustee and allocate powers as permitted by the plan document. However, with the exception of the power for the trustee to delegate fiduciary investment decisions (refer to discretionary vs. directed trustees in "A Prelude to Core Element 3"), the trustee generally cannot delegate their responsibilities.

Special rules also exist with regards to liability for multiple trustees. Multiple trustees are jointly and severally liable unless they are responsible for different pools of assets, as dictated by the documents.[19] For multiple trusts under a plan, the separate trustees are generally not liable for each other. None of these special trustee liability rules supersede the overarching liability of the named fiduciary in appointing other fiduciaries, or in the trustee's duty to the trust and ERISA.

TRAP #8

NOT UNDERSTANDING AND FOLLOWING A FIDUCIARY'S OBLIGATIONS UNDER ERISA

The single most critical failure for any ERISA fiduciary is them not understanding what their core duties are and to whom those duties correspond to. Failing to understand and follow these duties will blind you to proper decision making and greatly increase your liability as a fiduciary.

---

19 Grantz, Jason, and Samford, Michael. *Deconstructing the Discretionary Fiduciary Models: ERISA Section 3(38) Investment Managers vs. Discretionary Trustees.* PDF File.

The Core ERISA Fiduciary Duties

There are five basic duties for ERISA fiduciaries (technically four duties and one rule, but the distinction is not significant for the purposes of this book). These are the most important concepts to understand. I'm also going to cover an additional rule known as the "disclosure" rule, because it is a fiduciary responsibility even though it is not commonly sourced as one of the basic fiduciary duties.

The DOL is the primary regulation and enforcement body for fiduciary activities. It is important to understand that the DOL is very concerned with the processes of fiduciary decision making, not just the results. You will need to be able to demonstrate that correct and prudent processes were in place and followed, otherwise you could find yourself in trouble *even if the results themselves did not cause harm.*[20] Later in this section I will discuss more about the fiduciary decision making process and the best practices that the regulating agencies and the courts have previously found favorable to the fiduciary.

1. **You must discharge your plan duties for the exclusive purpose of providing benefits to the participants and beneficiaries, and pay only reasonable and necessary expenses.**

This is also known as the Exclusive Benefit or Exclusive Purpose rule. This rule is so important that it appears twice in ERISA and once in the IRC. The fiduciary must carry out this duty to the participants and beneficiaries to provide the intended benefits. It is important to understand that since expenses paid by the plan (and thus by the participants/beneficiaries) can have a significant impact on the benefits received, expenses paid by the plan must be evaluated to ensure they are reasonable and necessary and the plan's responsible fiduciary must consistently make that determination. The subject of monitoring and evaluating fees and service providers is covered in Core Element 3, "Service Provider Retention".

---

20   Swisher, Pete. 401(k) *Fiduciary Governance: An Advisors Guide. Arlington:*
ASPPA, 2012. Print.

2. **You must discharge your plan duties solely in the interest of the participants and beneficiaries, and avoid conflicts of interest (and prohibited transactions).**

This is also known as the Duty of Loyalty. At its core, any decision you make must only consider the interests of the participants and beneficiaries. You cannot make decisions that benefit the owners, the company, or any other person or entity above the participants and beneficiaries. Plan fiduciaries must consider the impact of any action, or lack thereof, on the participants and beneficiaries and exercise caution not to enter into any transaction that could be construed as detrimental to them.

It seems obvious that any transaction involving "self-dealing" to the detriment of the plan would be a conflict of interest, but many conflicts are not so readily apparent. There are a series of "prohibited transactions" whereby any fiduciary engaging in such action would be in violation of their duties unless they utilized an "exemption". Exemptions are specific to each transaction; prohibited transactions will be covered later in this section.

3. **You must act with the care, skill, prudence and diligence that a prudent person acting in a like capacity and familiar with such matters would use in the conduct of an enterprise with like character and aims.**

This is known as the Duty of Prudence or the Prudent Man Rule. In considering any fiduciary decisions, you must do it with careful consideration. This means you have to follow a diligent process, referred to as "procedural prudence". You must consider whether given facts and circumstances are relevant to any decision, and if so you must consider them in the decision making process. If there is a part of the process or evidence that you are not familiar or skilled with, you need to bring in experts to assist you.

Claiming ignorance of the process, information or materials will not protect a fiduciary from being found guilty of violating this rule, but adherence to procedural prudence will often (but not always) indemnify the fiduciary from harm as a result of a decision that resulted in any given outcome (good or bad). And yes, you just read that right: failure to follow a prudent process can cause liability for the fiduciary even if that outcome was beneficial to the plan.

This rule is of particular note because most plan sponsors are not "experts" in the fields of investments, ERISA, investment expense analysis, etc. Generally speaking the interpretations of the courts have been that, in the absence of in-house expertise, seeking expert consultation is a minimum requirement to remain compliant with the law.[21] However, reliance upon the advice of the expert does not indemnify the fiduciary from liability; in other words expert advice in and of itself does not demonstrate a prudent process, but is merely part of the process.

4. **You must follow the instruments and plan documents governing the plan, insofar as they are consistent with ERISA, but not if following the plan documents would be imprudent.**

This is known as the Duty of Obedience. This rule means that plan operation and governance is dictated by the plan documents, and any decision made by the fiduciary must be consistent with what the documents permit. The only exceptions are if the plan documents are in conflict with ERISA, or if following the plan document would be clearly imprudent for the given circumstance. That is why it is important to thoroughly draft, read and understand the plan documents before considering any decision that could be limited by those artifacts.

5. **Diversify investment options, unless it is clearly imprudent to do so.**

This is called the Duty to Diversify. It requires the plan sponsor to offer a broad range of investment choices to mitigate sudden, significant losses to plan assets, unless it is clearly imprudent to do so. ERISA and the DOL do not generally endorse any specific investment or class of

---

21 Reish, Fred, and Faucher, Joe. *The Fiduciary Duty to Ask for Help. Reish, Luftman, Reicher and Cohen.* PDF File.

investments; it is up to the responsible fiduciary to determine what investments are utilized and weigh the benefits and risks.

Due to the evolution of plan design over the years, especially in the area of participant investment direction, this is a less recognized rule because most plans offer dozens of investment choices that clearly satisfy the rule. Even more significant to this rule is section 404(c) which provides some legal protection to fiduciaries for the active investment decisions of the participants, provided that certain conditions are met. For more information on 404(c), see the Core Element 4 on "Investment Management".

Maintaining Transparency: The Disclosure Requirements

Even though disclosure rules are not commonly cited as one of the core fiduciary functions, it is nevertheless a fiduciary function and one of the cornerstones of ERISA law. The general rule is that the plan's administrator is the fiduciary responsible for ensuring both accuracy and timeliness of disclosures. The disclosure rules require the plan to report information to two groups: the regulating agencies (DOL, IRS, and PBGC) and the participants/beneficiaries. The required disclosure to the regulating agencies is the Form 5500 (or its various incarnations), which satisfies the reporting requirements for all government agencies.

Participant disclosures requirements have traditionally involved descriptions of the plan, rights, benefits, modifications, account statements, etc. However, new rules implemented in 2012 have changed the landscape of participant disclosure requirements and place a significant burden on the plan sponsor to ensure the both accuracy and timeliness of these reports, and by virtue of liability demand the employer create a documented process to protect themselves. For a thorough review of the requirements and recommended processes, see Core Element 5 "Administrative Management".

TRAP #9

ENGAGING IN PROHIBITED TRANSACTIONS

Engaging in a prohibited transaction is a fiduciary failure.
Prohibited transaction are a complex area of plan governance,
but ignorance of the basics of prohibited transactions will
likely result in you making decisions that could subject you
to enforcement or litigation.

Prohibited Transactions: A Fiduciary No-No

A prohibited transaction is a rule that says what you cannot do with plan assets and who you can't do it with. Transactions undertaken by the fiduciary that are prohibited would be a violation of their duties and will expose the fiduciary to civil and/or criminal penalties. This is governed by the nuance of ERISA law and includes many inherent conflicts of interest. The subject of prohibited transactions is the purview of attorneys, judges and scholars and will only be expounded upon to the extent of general education at this level.

There are many prohibited transactions that are common sense, but there are just as many that are not. But in many cases there exists "exemptions" to the rule. Understanding the basics of what you can and cannot do related to plan assets and management, and the corresponding exemptions, is a critically important aspect to any fiduciary decision making process.

I'm going to review a few of the most common prohibited transactions; this is by no means an exhaustive list, and in reviewing these it is my intention to expose you to prohibited transactions and exemptions and give you some insight into their functionality. First we need to review a definition of a "party in interest". A "party in interest" is generally a person or entity that is related to the plan. Parties in interest include:

A. Any fiduciary (including, but not limited to, any administrator, officer, trustee, or custodian), counsel, or employee of the plan;

B. A person providing services to the plan;

C. An employer, any of whose employees are covered by the plan;

D. An employee organization, any of whose members are covered by the plan;

E. An owner, direct or indirect, of 50% or more of:

    a. The combined voting power of all classes of stock entitled to vote or the total value of shares of all classes of stock of a corporation;

    b. The capital interest or profits interest of a partnership; or

    c. The beneficial interest of a trust or unincorporated enterprise which is an employer or an employee organization described in C or D;

F. A relative of any individual described in A, B, C, or E (the term "relative" means a spouse, ancestor, lineal descendant, or spouse of a lineal descendant);

G. A corporation, partnership, or trust or estate of which (or in which) 50% or more of:

    a. The combined voting power of all classes of stock entitled to vote or the total value of shares of all classes of stock of a corporation;

    b. The capital interest or profits interest of a partnership; or

    c. The beneficial interest of such trust or estate, is owned directly or indirectly, or held by persons described in A, B, C, D, or E;

H. An employee, officer, director (or an individual having powers or responsibilities similar to those of officers or directors), or a 10% or more shareholder directly or indirectly, of a person in B, C, D, E, or G, or of the employee benefit plan;

I. A 10% or more (directly or indirectly in capital or profits) partner of joint venturer of a person described in B, C, D, E, or G.

It is important to understand who may be a party in interest and what that means for a plan. Specifically, prohibited transactions mostly concern transactions between the plan and parties in interest.

Common Prohibited Transactions

In general, ERISA prohibits certain transactions between the plan and a party in interest, and conflicts of interest by plan fiduciaries. Exemptions do exist for certain situations involving some of these transactions; otherwise these prohibited transactions are so restrictive a retirement plan could not even function in its modern form. Absent an exemption, the following transactions between the plan and parties in interest are prohibited under ERISA:

- The sale, exchange, or lease of property between the plan and a party in interest;
- A loan or extension of credit between the plan and a party in interest;
- Furnishing of goods, services, or facilities between the plan and a party in interest;
- Transfer of plan assets to, or use by or for the benefit of a party in interest;
- Acquisition, on behalf of the plan, of any employer security or real property (in violation of section 1107a of ERISA).

Additionally, fiduciaries are prohibited from engaging in conflicts of interest, particularly:

- A fiduciary is prohibited from dealing with plan assets for his own benefit;
- A fiduciary is prohibited from representing an adverse party with respect to the plan.

Most prohibited transactions make sense; a fiduciary must not use plan assets for their own benefit, and must avoid conflicts of interest (the latter without exception and irrespective of the outcome). Upon reflection, such as the transaction related to the "transfer of any assets to a party in interest" it seems to say you cannot use plan assets for anyone "in interest" to the plan, including employers, employees, service providers, etc. And in fact, that is what it does say.

This approach is the opposite of what we commonly associate with substantive law in the United States; any transaction with a party in interest using the assets of an ERISA retirement plan is prohibited unless there is an exemption, as opposed to it being permitted unless there is a specific prohibition. It's essentially a blanket prohibition. So how can you hire someone to help manage the plan when you are expressly prohibited from doing so? Moreover, how does this plan provide benefits to an employee when its assets can't be used for their benefit? The answer lies with the aforementioned "exemption".

Exemptions exist to allow transactions to occur that would ordinarily be a violation of fiduciary responsibility under ERISA. For instance, fiduciaries can be paid for their services provided they meet the requirements for exemption (which precludes certain fiduciaries from receiving compensation, but not others). Additionally, plans can contract with service providers and pay them using plan assets, provided the exemptions are met. These exemptions provide a work around the highly prohibitive legislation as long as the exemption exists and its requirements are met.

The three basic types of exemptions are statutory, class and individual:

1. **Statutory** exemptions are written into the law, and permit the fiduciary to use plan assets in a transaction with a party in interest provided any requisite conditions are met. Examples include: allowing participants to take loans from their accounts, contracting a service provider, contracting with certain insurance companies, making bank deposits, etc. Statutory exemptions are detailed under ERISA 408(a).

2. **Class** exemptions are granted administratively by the DOL. Anyone meeting the criteria and conditions of the class exemption may engage in the transaction for which the exemption was granted.

3. **Individual** exemptions are granted by the DOL only for the individual making the request and do not extend to anyone else even if all applicable facts and circumstances are the same.

Exemptions exist for all manner of situations, so an exhaustive list of exemptions is beyond the scope of this book, but you can find a list of statutory exemptions under 29 U.S.C. §1108, and a list of class exemptions can be found at www.dol.gov/ebsa/Regs/ClassExemptions/main.html.

Consequences of Breaching Your Fiduciary Duty

The consequences for a fiduciary breach are significant and should be clearly understood; therefore you should first know to whom you may be responsible to. For a fiduciary breach resulting in damages, remedy can be sought and recovered by the plan participants, beneficiaries and/or the DOL. For fiduciary breaches not resulting in damages, the DOL can initiate action and recover fines. The IRS has the power to seek remedy for breaches of the Internal Revenue Code and can also levy fines.

In the most egregious of situation, the IRS can disqualify the tax status of the plan resulting in all plan assets being countable to each participant's ordinary income (to the extent that they are attributable to the participant and pre-tax) in the year the plan was disqualified with no future tax deferral applicable. Although not common in execution, this power none the less exists.

Fiduciaries are *personally liable* for their actions;[22] plan assets cannot be used to pay for mistakes. Fiduciaries are always personally liable for actions due to gross negligence and/or willful misconduct, but even absent of that you may not always rely on corporate indemnification for individuals, owners, or otherwise. Criminal penalties include fines up to $100,000 and 10 years imprisonment for individuals, and up to

---

22 Wagner, Marcia. *A Plan Sponsor's Fiduciary Duties Under ERISA: With Great Responsibility Comes Great Potential Liability.* The Wagner Law Group. 2010. PDF File.

$500,000 for "non-individuals". Civil penalties range from $100 per day per violation to $1,000 per day.[23] Additionally, the IRS can levy excise taxes up to 15% of the amount in question, and the DOL can enforce a penalty of up to 20% for fiduciary violations, in addition to demanding the restoration of any losses to the plan with interest.

In the past, the courts and the DOL have sought and won from individual (or groups of) fiduciaries:

• Restoration of losses, including remedy for lost investment opportunity.

• Relinquishment of profits.

• Civil penalties.

• Criminal prosecution.

• Removal of fiduciaries, barring persons from acting as an ERISA fiduciary, and appointing an independent third party as a plan fiduciary.

• Additional penalties.

EBSA, the enforcement arm of the DOL, reports annually on the results of investigations covered by the DOL. For the fiscal year 2013:[24]

• Civil Investigations
    • 3,677 cases closed
    • 2,677 cases closed with results (72.8%)
    • 190 cases referred for litigation
    • 111 cases with litigation filed

• Criminal Investigations
    • 320 cases closed

---

23 William Gallagher Associates. *What Can Noncompliance Cost You?* PDF File.

24 Employee Benefits Security Administration. (2014). *Fact Sheet: EBSA Achieves Over $1.6 Billion in Total Monetary Results in Fiscal Year 2013.* Retrieved from United States Department of Labor: www.dol.gov/ebsa/newsroom/fsFYagencyresults.html

• Monetary Results

  • $911.3 M prohibited transaction/plan assets protected
  • $423.6 M plan assets restored/participant benefits recovered
  • $72.1 M voluntary fiduciary correction programs
  • **$1.69 Billion total monetary results**

TRAP #10

NOT CORRECTING
FIDUCIARY FAILURES PROPERLY

When prohibited transactions occur, the most important thing to do is to first identify that it had taken place, then take steps to remedy it. Nothing will get you in deeper trouble faster than trying to sweep these failures under the rug. Knowing what to do is critical to minimizing the liability of litigation or enforcement. Fortunately, the governing agencies anticipate that these failures will occur and have processes in place for correction.

I Messed Up, What Should I Do Now?

Like any violation of fiduciary responsibility, the consequences are *real* and *personal*. This includes civil penalties such as excise taxes, penalties, recoupment, up to and including criminal prosecution and imprisonment. The worst thing you can do is attempt to engage in any action of willful deceit. As with anything of legal consequence, you should first consider contacting an attorney with intimate familiarity of ERISA for instructions on how to proceed given a specific set of circumstances, but I'll cover the broad overview of what can and often is done.

When a fiduciary engages in a prohibited transaction, the first thing to do is recognize that a prohibited transaction has taken place. Next, **contact an attorney who specializes in ERISA issues.** Make sure you *personally "contract" with the attorney*, versus the attorney contracting with the plan, and *be wary about using plan assets to pay legal fees*. Courts have poked holes in attorney-client privilege for ERISA matters when the attorney is contracted by the plan (or is paid for by the plan) as opposed to contracting with and paid by the fiduciary whose compliance with the law is in question.[25]

Regardless of whether the prohibited transaction is directly attributable to the discovering fiduciary OR to another fiduciary, immediate action should be taken (not necessarily in this order and *only upon consultation with a competent legal professional*):

1. **End** the prohibited transaction immediately;
2. **Notify** other plan fiduciaries of the infraction and coordinate to determine the extent;
3. **Analyze** the nature of the infraction and determine any and all fiduciaries who had any discretion or control related to the offense;
4. **Determine** if any available self-correcting remedies are applicable;
5. **Follow** the applicable correction program requirements;
6. **Restore** the plan whole, with interest, as if it had never happened;
7. **Disclose** to the regulating agency(s).

Simply removing the at-fault fiduciary will not comply with your obligations. For instance, if you contract a fiduciary service provider to the plan and they uncover a prohibited transaction by another fiduciary, they might be obligated by ERISA to report the prohibited transaction to the appropriate agency. Thus it behooves a plan's fiduciaries to monitor for and avoid prohibited transactions at all costs.

Depending on the nature of the transaction, you may have several remedies available to you. For certain transactions involving securities or commodities, a 14 day safe harbor for excise taxes is available, if the

---

25   Center for Due Diligence. *Fiduciary Liability and E&O Insurance for ERISA Plans: Most Don't Have It.* Western Springs: CFDD, 2009. PDF File.

transaction is corrected within the time and the date the violation was discovered or should have been discovered.

There is a program made available by the DOL referred to as the Voluntary Fiduciary Correction Program, or VFCP.[26] For certain transactions outlined under the program, remedies exist that allow the plan fiduciary to correct the transaction based on rules for correction, eligibility and application specific to each transactional violation. VFCP may also provide relief from excise taxes, and is usually the best course of action if it is available (see the section on Core Element Five "Administration"). Finally, the plan sponsor must report non-exempt transactions with parties in interest on the IRS form 5500 annually or face possibly severe penalties.

An attorney experienced with such matters can help you navigate through the potential remedies. Be warned that failure to respond with appropriate action, both proactively and retroactively can result in severe consequences as already discussed.

Best Practices

P³: Policies, Processes and Procedures

Understanding policies, processes and procedures and implementing them properly are critical to core fiduciary responsibilities. Let's briefly explore the difference:[27]

- **Policy:** Policies are the overriding rules and guidelines. Processes and procedures are developed from policies. Policies address *what it is, who is responsible for enforcement, and why it is necessary.* In the context of ERISA fiduciary controls, ERISA legislation and DOL regulation and advisory opinions primarily dictate policy, so understanding the roles and responsibilities under the law and

---

26   www.dol.gov/ebsa/newsroom/fs2006vfcp.html.

27   KCG Consultant Group, I. (2010). *Policy, Process and Procedure - What's the Difference?* Retrieved from KCG Consultant Group, Inc.: kcggroup.com/PoliciesProcessesProcedureDifferences

regulatory environment is a critical function. Policies can and often are incorporated for investment management, service provider retention, and educational requirements for retirement plans.

- **Process:** Processes address the steps necessary to fulfill requirements under the policies. Processes address who is responsible to perform the process, what functions are performed, and when the process is triggered. Unlike policies, processes may or may not exist under the law. You may find regulatory opinions and best practices for processes.

- **Procedure:** Procedures deal with the specific instructions to comply with the process, such as what steps are performed, when they are performed incorporating legal or regulatory deadlines, and how they are performed. Procedures are where detail meets action.

By carefully addressing the policies, processes and procedures required for any given circumstance or event related to plan management, plan fiduciaries can greatly improve outcomes and deliver consistency in decision making processes. It is often useful to map out how these functions relate to one another and describing *who, what, when, where, why, and how at each level.*

TRAP #11

POOR FIDUCIARY GOVERNANCE

Processes need to be in place for the identification, appointment and removal of fiduciaries, as well as allocating and delegating responsibilities. This is an all too common failure in many plans, and one easily avoided.

Fiduciary Governance

The first step in good governance requires the plan to determine who the fiduciaries are. Remember that fiduciaries do not necessarily have to be named in the plan's documents; they can be deemed fiduciaries by the extent of their control over management or administration of the plan or plan assets, or by giving advice. So it is important to evaluate every person involved with the plan at those levels, and determine if there are any "un-intended" fiduciaries.

Next, ensure that the fiduciaries in charge are qualified to perform that role. Qualification requirements should include at a minimum: criminal background checks (ERISA prohibits people with convictions for certain types of crimes from being a fiduciary for a period of time)[28], experience working with retirement plans, experience with the specific duty requirements, knowledge of ERISA provisions, and applicable designations or education. Remember, the plan's named fiduciary has the responsibility to vet and select other fiduciaries.

If there are multiple fiduciaries, you should clearly define the roles and responsibilities of each fiduciary. This is a critical part of the process, because you don't want to commit a prohibited transaction because you had two plan administrators who each thought the other "had it covered". In that case, they both may be liable. The delineation of roles and responsibilities should be spelled out clearly in writing. In the process of determining these matters, you should begin to see a clear picture of hierarchy between the fiduciaries. Determining this hierarchy will help you implement more internal control procedures outlined below.[29]

Next, create procedures for delegation of responsibility, follow up, and performance assessment. If responsibility is delegated, it's important for the fiduciary with overarching responsibility to have a procedure in place for ensuring the delegated responsibility is actually fulfilled.

---

28   www.dol.gov/ebsa/oemanual/cha47.html

29   Swisher, Pete. 401(k) *Fiduciary Governance: An Advisors Guide.* Arlington: ASPPA, 2012. Print.

This requires a communication plan and protocols for each delegation, including deadlines preferably ahead of statutory deadlines to allow some flexibility as needed. Performance assessment goes hand in hand with determining the success of delegation. Metrics for performance may include determining whether deadlines were met, innovation, the discovery of potential problems and overall success of delegation.

Finally, have a plan in place for removal and replacement of fiduciaries. Plan fiduciaries can "resign" from their duties or be removed. For fiduciaries who resign, having a clear understanding of their delegated responsibilities will aid the overarching fiduciary in determining what needs to be done to ensure continuity. The decision to remove a fiduciary is much more serious. Care should be taken to evaluate what metrics may lead to such a decision. In either event, a procedure should be in place to analyze the work of the resigned/removed fiduciary to ensure no prohibited transactions took place under their watch.

This seems like a lot of work to provide for basic procedures, and it is. Remember, the named fiduciary has the responsibility for selecting and monitoring other fiduciaries. If possible, utilize in-house committees to provide oversight and assist you in the process. Committees can be named as fiduciaries also. The more eyes you have, the more likely you'll catch something. I would provide a template for these procedures, but each plan can be vastly different in structure, therefore no one outline would work for more than a few plans. But we can summarize as follows:[30]

- Identify all named and functional fiduciaries.
- Determine qualifications for selection.
- Determine and/or define roles and responsibilities for each fiduciary.
- Create process for delegation and follow up.
- Create a performance assessment procedure for monitoring fiduciaries and delegated responsibilities.

---

30 Swisher, Pete. *401(k) Fiduciary Governance: An Advisors Guide*. Arlington: ASPPA, 2012. Print.

- Have a procedure in place for fiduciaries who resign, and metrics and procedures for removing fiduciaries.

TRAP #12

NOT FOLLOWING A PRUDENT, DOCUMENTED FIDUCIARY PROCESS

Having proper processes and procedures for making fiduciary decisions is one of the most common failures cited in litigation and enforcement action. Equally important is documenting the process. Failure to document the steps taken, information considered, and reasons for decisions is equivalent to not having a process at all because you will not be able to prove you had a process, much less followed it.

Procedural Prudence

The process of procedure prudence is not clearly defined in ERISA, therefore we can summarize best practices based on a conglomeration of industry best practices, case law, and advisory opinions by the DOL. Procedural prudence should be implemented in all decision making practices for retirement plans. The procedure I will propose is a seven step process.

1. *Determine if the decision is a fiduciary or settlor decision.*

This is the most important question to ask first, because if it is not a fiduciary decision, procedural prudence may not be required. Settlor decisions are by definition not fiduciary in nature. Therefore if you determine that the decision is a settlor decision, it should be made by the plan sponsor and the rest of these procedures need not be adhered to although good governance may incorporate some or all of these steps. The question to ask is "Is this a settlor decision?" since settlor decisions are much narrower in number and scope.[31] Sometimes, it may not be entirely clear whether it is a settlor decision or not; even courts have wrestled with some of the particulars on this subject. If you are unsure, you should consult an attorney familiar with ERISA.

2. Determine who is authorized to make that decision.

If the decision is fiduciary in nature, you should determine under whose authority it falls. Generally speaking, "trustee" fiduciary decisions involve plan assets and (maybe) investments; and "administrator" fiduciary decisions involve administrative, reporting and disclosure requirements. But the actual determination of who's responsible for the decision should be clear if the preceding steps of fiduciary governance are adhered to.

3. Determine what information is required to analyze and make a decision in the best interest of the plan's participants.

This step goes to the heart of the Exclusive Benefit and Prudent Man Rules. If you don't know what information you need to evaluate in order to make a decision for the exclusive benefit of the participants, how can you prudently justify making any decision at all? So this step may seem somewhat ambiguous at first, but upon the application of a specific decision to this step you should begin to see what information should be considered. If you need assistance consult your advisor or an attorney to help you determine what information may actually be relevant to the decision.

4. Gather the information required to assist in the decision making process.

Until recently getting access to information related to particular decisions, such as whether to retain services, was not always a straightforward process. For decisions like service provider retention, certain disclosures are now required by law, and remedies and consequences are prescribed for those who refuse to disclose that

---

31 Employee Benefits Security Administration. (n.d.). *Guidance on Settlor v. Plan Expenses*. Retrieved from United States Department of Labor: www.dol.gov/ebsa/ regs/AOs/settlor_guidance.html

information to plan fiduciaries. I'll cover that specific circumstance in another section, but rest assured you need to make every effort to obtain the information you need to make the decision. If someone withholds information, a great weight should be placed on that lack of transparency, it should be documented, and consideration should be given as to whether to continue a relationship with that service provider.

Some information may already be available in-house or through contracted vendors. A good fiduciary documentation calendar should be utilized to communicate to other providers for access to records and for your own responsibilities. These calendars provide important dates for required disclosures, testing and other important deadlines and are available on the web or through one or all of your service providers, particularly administrative service providers. Having a process in place to get copies of important documents from your vendors can assist you when it comes time to gather information relevant to a decision.

5. Analyze the information, and if you need assistance you have a duty to ask for it from an expert.

This step is critical, because it truly is the heart of prudence. Proper analysis of relevant information to affect decision making is crucial. This is the one step where consultation with experts, in-house and outside, is the responsibility of the fiduciary in charge. The prudent man rule demands it. So if you have trouble deciphering the information, or if you are not yourself an expert in these issues, you must consult those who are.

6. Formulate a decision and implement an action plan.

Taking into account the core fiduciary duties, a decision must be arrived at even if that decision is not to make any changes. Once a decision is made, you need to create an action plan to implement the decision if there will be any changes to the plan. Again, consultation with an expert in this area can help you tremendously in determining what steps need to be taken, in what order and when, to properly modify the plan.

7. Document the process, retain records related to relevant information gathered, and justify the decision in writing.

I cannot emphasize how important it is to document everything. In the eyes of the DOL, if a decision is not properly documented, no assumption may be made as to its prudence, therefore the default position may be to assume imprudence. Think of it like your medical records: If a surgical procedure is not in your records, the default assumption is that you haven't had it. Now you may know what you did and what efforts were made, but in absence of a documented process, with evidence and justification of disposition, you are inviting the DOL or the courts to make their own interpretation of what due diligence was followed or not. Don't leave it up to interpretation: Document it!

The Fiduciary File

We recommend that plan fiduciaries keep and maintain a "fiduciary file" containing documents relevant to plan functions. This file should be updated throughout the plan year and contain only documentation relevant to the plan for any given year, with a separate file maintained for each "plan year". A thorough, well managed and organized fiduciary file serves as the first line of defense against legal or regulatory action.

The fiduciary file should contain all plan related documents (master document, adoption agreement and/or trust documents), regulatory filings, ledgers from service providers, participant related documents, bonding and insurance contracts, service providers agreements with evidence of due diligence and fee analysis, investment related documents, compliance testing results and corrections, and agendas, minutes of meetings, and related documentation regarding fiduciary meetings and decisions.

Fiduciary Education

It is the opinion of this author that failing to educate yourself and other plan fiduciaries about their responsibilities under ERISA is a failure of prudence. I am not aware of any case law justifying my position, but I think it is just a matter of time before some "unintended fiduciary" who becomes liable as a result of their misunderstanding successfully sues another fiduciary for failing to provide the necessary guidance and education.

To that effect, you should consider a fiduciary education program with specific topics discussed at regular intervals and documented attendance and participation. It should also include education on relevant legislative changes, advisory opinions, and/or case law. Plan level advisors and consultants can assist you with this. Additionally, having an advisor, consultant or legal counsel as a non-voting committee member for plan committees can be a great service to the plan.[32]

TRAP #13

NOT HAVING THE PROPER
FIDUCIARY BONDING AND INSURANCE

It's remarkable how many plans we see that do not have the appropriate bonding in place, and bonding (or lack thereof) is reportable in required disclosures to the regulating agencies. It's a warning sign to an auditor that you may need an examination of your processes. Although insurance is not reportable, it's a key component for minimizing financial liability.

---

32 Roberts, J., & Treichel, B. (n.d.). *Fiduciary Governance: Challenges and Opportunities.* Pension Resource Institute.

Bonding and Insurance

There are two basic types of protections: fidelity bonds and insurance. Fidelity bonds are the easiest to understand. Fidelity bonds protect plan assets in the event of malfeasance by a person(s) with access to those assets. Fidelity bonds are required by ERISA and conform to specific requirements from selected vendors. It is against the law for plan officials or any other un-bonded persons from exercising control or custody of plan assets. In general, all plan officials, fiduciaries and anyone who handles plan funds must be bonded (this can include the person in the payroll department who segregates contributions from participants). The DOL has issued guidance by way of FAB 2008-4 regarding the subject of bonding, and you should consult it for further clarification. Fidelity bonds must be declared on the 5500 filing and can trigger an audit if undisclosed. Minimum bonding requirements are:

- Ten percent of plan assets, no less than $1,000 up to $500,000, determined at the beginning of the plan year;

- Plan's that hold "non-qualified" assets such as certain employer securities are subject to different bonding requirements.

There are several types of insurances available as well. Plans can purchase liability insurance for fiduciaries, *but if plan assets are used to purchase the insurance it must provide for recourse against the fiduciaries.* Individual fiduciary liability policies can be purchased to cover fiduciaries as long as they are not paid for using plan assets. Other types of insurance, such as errors and omissions (E&O) or director and officer (D&O) insurances may have a role to play. You should consult with an advisor or insurance agent with experience with these types of policies.

Hiring an Independent Fiduciary

In some situations, it may be prudent to hire an individual or entity to act as a fiduciary that is independent to the plan fiduciaries, the company and its officers. These situations may include transactions related to employer stock, sale-leaseback plan investments, and any other situation where the plan fiduciaries are confronted with a decision that may represent a conflict of interest.[33]

Read the Fine Print: Fiduciary Warranties

There are a number of service providers offering "fiduciary warranties" in lieu of defined fiduciary or co-fiduciary services. You should exercise caution when examining these warranties; some of them are legally stripped down to provide very little protection for the holder. Some limited scope warranties only provide protection if the plan's fiduciaries strictly follow their template, and often clearly indicate that the issuer does not assume any fiduciary responsibility for the plan.

Never automatically assume these warranties are indemnifying the fiduciary from liability. Some fiduciary warranties contain exculpatory language that omits the warranty for certain types of claims, often the ones you would most likely face. Fiduciary warranties come in many flavors and types they should be carefully scrutinized by an expert because in some cases they provide little, if any protection at all. An attorney specializing in ERISA law can help, but understand that the fiduciary warranty was initially designed to serve as a marketing tool for the service provider and may provide only limited or non-existent indemnification of liability for the plan's fiduciaries.

---

33 Halpern, S. (2014). *Role of the Independent Fiduciary*. Arthur J. Gallagher and Co.

Summary

In this section we learned that fiduciaries under ERISA have specific and precise responsibilities to the plan and its participants. Distinguishing which decisions are fiduciary in nature and which are not (settlor decisions) is crucial to understanding the application of the law with respect to fiduciary duties. Following a process of procedural prudence is the method for determining how decisions should be made. Failing to adhere to your legal responsibilities can cause a fiduciary to be personally liable for correcting any mistakes, restoring losses, and paying fines, taxes and/or restitution.

The best way to protect yourself is to follow a process designed to take into account the various facts and circumstances of any action with respect to your fiduciary responsibilities. Seeking expert advice is implied as part of due diligence if you lack the expertise in-house, and documenting the process is equally important should you ever need to demonstrate to a regulatory body, adversarial attorney or court of law that you followed a process designed to protect the participants and beneficiaries from harm.

A PRIMER FOR
CORE ELEMENT 3:
THE ROLES OF
SERVICE PROVIDERS

THE STORY...

A local Third Party Administrator that I work with, and have tremendous respect for, informed me of an interesting situation she had run across recently. She had been asked by another advisor to examine the plan design for a local professional medical services business. The business had a bundled 401(k) plan with a very large, well known service provider.

Upon examining the census and current plan design, she made a startling discovery. The current bundled provider had created a situation in which the plan was going to fail a key compliance test, and as a result the business owner was going to be on the hook for almost $50,000 in excise taxes and penalties. Nevertheless, her experience led her to dig deeper and she subsequently discovered an obvious, glaring error made by the current service provider that created the impending tax disaster.

Amazing, this error was so obvious and preventable that it's hard to believe such a large service provider, well known to anyone in the business, could cause such a situation in the first place. She met with the owners and informed them of the news, what had been done wrong, and that it was correctable with the right guidance. The business owner immediately contracted with the discovering TPA and initiated an inquiry for new service providers in an effort to terminate services from the existing vendor.

The end result was that the errors were corrected in time, the business owner avoided the tax disaster and possible plan disqualification, and contracted with new service providers including the TPA that helped fix the problem, and now has well managed plan providing a great benefit for him and his employees.

＊＊

There are many different potential players when it comes to servicing a retirement plan, and understanding who does what is an important first step in knowing what services you may want to contract for the plan, and what services and vendors you won't want. The goals of this section are to:

✓ Acknowledge the source of significant confusion for plan
   fiduciaries when it comes to service providers;
✓ Define all the names, roles and responsibilities of all
   fiduciaries that are typically found in a retirement plan;
✓ Define all the names, roles and responsibilities of any service
   providers that may be associated with a retirement plan.

TRAP #14

NOT UNDERSTANDING THE ROLES AND RESPONSIBILITIES OF THE DIFFERENT SERVICE PROVIDERS

There are a variety of different entities that can be contracted for services to a plan, but often plan officials are not entirely clear about exactly what the roles and responsibilities of these different vendors are. Not understanding who is responsible for what can lead to confusion, miscommunication and ultimately fiduciary failures.

The Confusion

Understanding the differentiation between titles, roles and responsibilities is part of what a good business owner does every day, but those same strengths fail them in the area of plan governance. The reason is probably twofold: the roles can be confusing (especially when several roles are provided by the same person or entity), and no one bothered to ever show them the difference. But it is critical to understand the segregation of duties and responsibilities, because as the plan sponsor it's your responsibility to know.

Even more critical is the understanding of who, by will or consequence, is a co-fiduciary and who is not because service providers will deny a fiduciary role if not expressed in writing, and sometimes even if a written acknowledgment seems to confirm it (see "Fiduciary Warranties" at the end of Core Element Two, "Fiduciary Controls"). After you finish this section, you'll be able to identify and distinguish the basic roles and responsibilities of each title.

The Plan Sponsor

The plan sponsor is the entity/employer that sponsors the retirement plan. It can be a corporation, partnership or a sole proprietor. It can also be a government or municipal entity, a non-profit, or a religious institution. There are even plans that are adopted under multiple employer arrangements.

As mentioned previously, the plan sponsor acts in a settlor capacity by creating the plan's terms and conditions, executing a document describing those terms and conditions, and providing a procedure for making amendments. The plan sponsor also has the authority to start or terminate a plan or amend a plan's design features. Although the title "plan sponsor" does not imply fiduciary, often they are a fiduciary because they fall under another category below. This leads to the problem of "wearing two hats".

The "two hat" problem results when a person or persons have multiple roles and responsibilities that are legally distinct from each other. It is critical to be able to distinguish your roles and that can be done relatively easily with the right understanding and guidance. Failure to distinguish these roles can result in fiduciary failures in decision making, implementation, and operations. The most common source of problems results from the distinction between fiduciary and settlor roles. The key to working around the problem of wearing "two hats" is to follow a process of procedural prudence as outlined in the last section.

Named Fiduciaries in the Plan Documents

A named fiduciary is any person, committee or entity named as a fiduciary with respect to the plan in the plan documents. At least one named fiduciary must be specifically assigned in the plan documents. Most often the named fiduciary will be an individual, usually an owner, partner, or officer affiliated with the plan sponsor.

Occasionally committees may be named, but the committee should be designed so that individuals with voting privileges cannot force inaction as the result of the inability to reach a consensus. There can and probably should be non-voting committee members (typically employees, advisors, and legal/tax professionals) with particular skills or insight to provide some guidance or clarification to questions presented to the committee. Non-voting members generally have no fiduciary liability because they do not exercise decision making control due to their non-voting status.

It is not uncommon to see an entity as a named fiduciary. Although some companies still have a named fiduciary as the company, ERISA generally does not recognize corporate indemnification from individual liability under the law, and the person(s) responsible for fulfilling the role of the named fiduciary will hold the liability for their actions. In a recent court case, the "company" was the named fiduciary in the plan documents accused of withholding contributions, and because the CEO's signature could authorize bank transactions, the CEO was found to be a fiduciary.[34] We also sometimes see third party entities as named fiduciaries.

ERISA identifies four categories of named fiduciaries: Plan Sponsor, Plan Administrator, Trustee (Discretionary only), and Investment Manager.

The Plan Administrator

The Plan Administrator is one of the most commonly confused and misunderstood titles.

The plan administrator is responsible for managing the plan according to the plan documents, providing disclosures to participants and beneficiaries, reporting to IRS/DOL/PBGC, and any other responsibility set forth in the plan documents. Essentially the administrator is responsible for the day-to-day operations of the plan.

The administrator is always an ERISA fiduciary, and if no one is named as the administrator in the plan documents the position defaults to the plan sponsor.[35] Depending on the authority given to them, they may also be responsible for the decision to retain service providers to the plan. The plan administrator is one of the most important fiduciary roles to understand.

The Trustee

Qualified plan assets must be segregated from the general assets of the plan sponsor. Those assets are generally required to be held in a trust, with limited exceptions such as when assets are held in separate

---

34 Moore, R. (2014, Sept). *Signature Authority May Trigger ERISA Fiduciary Status* . Retrieved from PlanAdviser: www.planadviser.com/ Signature_Authority_May_Trigger_ERISA_Fiduciary_Status.aspx

35 Jackson, C., Kallstrom, D. W., & Martin, A. (2010). *Who May Sue You and Why: How to Reduce Your ERISA Risks, and the Role of Fiduciary Liability Insurance.* Warren: Chubb Group of Insurance Companies.

accounts with an insurance company. The trustee is the individual or entity responsible for safekeeping and managing the assets in trust for the benefit of the participants and beneficiaries. The trustee manages contributions into and distributions out of the trust.

The trustee is always an ERISA fiduciary (a special case for directed trustees to follow). The trustee is usually either the sponsoring employer (self-trustee) or a third party entity, such as a bank, insurance company, or other financial institution (corporate trustee). If the employer chooses to be the trustee, careful consideration must be made to determine if the company has people qualified to fill that role. If it is not qualified then it should consider training or hiring someone who is, or retain third party services.

A trustee can be either "discretionary" or "directed".

Directed Trustees

Directed trustees have no responsibility for the investment window; their job is solely to act in the role of trustee with regards to the assets of the trust, not the investment allocation. This generally means determining requests are in good order for movement of assets into or out of the trust, preventing prohibited transactions, and generally following the rules of an ERISA fiduciary. It's important to note that directed trustees are have been absolved in courts of any fiduciary responsibility to the investment window.[36]

Some directed trustees may not acknowledge ERISA fiduciary status, due in part to the lack of discretionary control which may remain with the plan sponsor with regards to direction of the assets of the trust. However, the directed trustee still has the responsibility to take only instructions consistent with ERISA and have functional "control" over assets, as a direct result of their title and position.

---

36 St. Martin, A. (2005). *Fiduciary Issues in ERISA-Covered Plans*. Groom Law Group.

Discretionary Trustees

Discretionary trustees have the additional responsibility to manage the investment window. They have the same function as the directed trustee with the added responsibility for the investments. They make decisions regarding the investments in the trust. Additionally, a discretionary trustee may delegate the responsibility of the investment window to an investment manager by contractual arrangement. This is the only allocation of responsibility permitted for a trustee of retirement plan assets. In any event, like the hiring of any co-fiduciary, the appointing fiduciary ultimately bears responsibility for their appointment and oversight.

It should be noted that the most common practice in the micro-medium size plan demographic is for the plan sponsor to hold numerous positions of authority in the plan, such as the administrator and trustee. Because the plan sponsor (the company's owners for instance) are also usually contributing to the plan, they are also participants and beneficiaries. Thus, an inherent conflict of interest exists and more importantly a murky distinction between the roles and responsibilities of each position, which usually leads to poor plan governance. However, the economics of scale often force smaller plans to assume these multiple roles. For plan sponsors who choose this path, it is critical that you understand the different roles, delineate the decision making processes accordingly, and get expert help as you go along.

The Custodian

The custodian is the entity that actually holds the assets of the plan. The custodian's responsibility is to house the assets, protect them from unauthorized access, collect interest/dividends earned, or other functions as prescribed. The custodian is always a bank, brokerage, insurance company or other financial institution.

In many cases the custodian and the trustee are the same. When they are not the same, the custodian then takes direction from the trustee but otherwise will make no decision regarding the assets of the plan.

Since a custodian makes no decisions about the plan, the custodian is generally not considered an ERISA fiduciary.[37]

The Investment Advisor/Manager

The investment manager or advisor makes decisions or provides advice regarding the investment options available to the participants in the plan. Investment management comes in two forms:

- 3(38) ERISA Discretionary Investment Manager: This type of investment manager has total control and discretion over the investment window offered by the plan. They have the absolute authority to make investment lineup decisions while retained. They direct the trustee regarding the suitability of investment options available in the plan and make changes as necessary. The 3(38) is always an ERISA fiduciary. This is the highest level of outsourcing for fiduciary investments decisions.

- 3(21)(A)(ii) ERISA Investment Advisor: An investment advisor has "non-discretionary" authority over plan investments; in other words they "advise" on investment decisions available in the plan, but they have no authority to direct changes themselves. Although these advisors will commonly acknowledge their role as an ERISA fiduciary, due to their lack of control the extent of their fiduciary liability is somewhat unclear, apart from the dereliction of their duties outlined by ERISA as a fiduciary. There are generally two variations of investment advisors, depending on who they are giving advice to:

  - Plan Level Advisors: These advisors provide advice to the responsible plan fiduciary regarding the selection and monitoring of the investments used or made available in the plan.

---

37 Goodwin Procter. (2012). Sixth Circuit Holds That ERISA Preempts State Law Claims Against Nonfiduciary Plan Custodian. *ERISA Litigation Update.*

- Participant Level Advisors: These advisors provide specific investment advice to plan participants and beneficiaries regarding their individual investment selections in participant directed accounts.

An advisor can be both plan and participant level, but ERISA imposes certain restrictions on advisors providing investment advice to participants. Under the Pension Protection Act of 2006 (PPA), in order to avoid a prohibited transaction a participant level advisor must either receive level compensation that does not vary based on the advice given, or if they receive variable compensation they must use an approved computer model that meets certain requirements under the provisions of the PPA. Additionally, most advisors will have to comply with a specific annual audit requirement which can be costly since there are currently only a few entities that are qualified to certify such an audit.

From a plan fiduciary's perspective, an investment advisor that offers specific investment advice to plan participants as part of their contract with the plan should comply with one of the two exemptions under the PPA. The plan fiduciary responsible for contracting with the investment advisor should make sure they understand that the advisor will comply with one of the PPA exemptions.

While the responsible plan fiduciary has the right to permit or prohibit participant level advisory services, the DOL has expressed its opinion that the plan fiduciary does NOT have a duty to monitor the advice given to participants unless participants complain about the advice they are being given. Currently, many investment advisors shy away from offering participant level advice because of uncertainty in the regulatory environment (new rules regarding participant advice are expected sometime in 2015).

Having one type of investment manager or advisor does not mutually exclude the use of the other. In fact, it is not uncommon to find both a 3(38) manager and 3(21)(A)(ii) advisor on the plan. In this role, typically the 3(38) manager narrows down a sleeve of approved funds which are monitored and replaced by the 3(38), while the 3(21)(A)(ii) advisor helps the responsible fiduciary narrow down a fund window appropriate for the plan's demographics and needs.

It's important to note that investment managers/advisors are not required; plan sponsors can retain total control of investment selection and oversight (usually by committee). A word of caution: if you retain this control in house make sure you have the proper expertise to do so.

The Record Keeper

The record keeper is responsible for tracking and allocating contributions and distributions, gains and losses, investment allocations, and expenses among other things. Record keepers are usually mutual fund companies, insurance companies, or other financial entities. The record keeper will usually provide the enrollment kits for participants, website access, and ongoing education (usually provided in person or online). Recordkeeping services typically charge based on the number of participants, the average account balance, or some combination. Record keeper services typically come "bundled" or "unbundled".

In bundled arrangements the record keeper will generally provide most services required for the plan, and in some cases they'll provide all required services for the plan. The benefits of a bundled arrangement include a single point of contact, simplified structure and generally lower costs due to discounted group service. The drawbacks include inability to separate services, often limited investment options, limited flexibility for more complex arrangements or services, and increasing scrutiny by regulating agencies.

Recently regulators have increased their attention to some of these arrangements due to the complexity of their fee arrangements, so exercise caution and diligence when examining bundled arrangements. For example, a bundled program may offer free recordkeeping services but charge above market rate investment or administrative fees, or receive other more complex forms of remuneration from other services. However, there are many good bundled arrangements available that may make sense for your plan, you just need to pay attention to the details and get good advice.

With unbundled recordkeeping services, you are contracting recordkeeping services and possibly other services, but not a "one-stop-shop". Other required services that are not provided with the unbundled arrangement will have to be hired separately. The benefits of unbundled arrangements are that they allow you to contract services independently, offer greater flexibility, flexible investment options, and easier expense itemization. The drawbacks include multiple points of contact, complexity and possibly greater expenses due to the segregation of services.

It is important to note that several courts have repeatedly determined that record keeper functions are ministerial and thus not fiduciary in nature.[38] Recordkeeping can be retained in house, but in almost all cases it is outsourced to a vendor with the requisite expertise.

The Third Party Administrator

A third party administrator (TPA) is responsible for complex calculations necessary to maintain IRS compliance. They essentially take the government reporting requirements out of the hands of the plan administrator, but they generally do not take any of the fiduciary liability. TPAs offer a variety of services and can vary significantly from one to the other and often include 5500 preparation, testing services, QDRO and loan management, participant notifications, and more. TPAs can help construct complex plan designs, profit sharing arrangements, and even other non-qualified compensation structures.

A good TPA can also be a first line of defense against an IRS or DOL audit. A bad TPA can cause nightmares for plan sponsors. TPA services are very important and should always be outsourced to an experienced

---

38 Mercado, D. (2014). 401(k) fiduciary lawsuit raises questions on record keeping. *Investment News*.

and competent firm unless the plan sponsor has the technically skilled in house resources to manage the complex administrative issues, which is rare.

The 3(16) Administrator

Although less common, some companies offer administrative services as a co-fiduciary, often taking most of the fiduciary responsibility for administration away from the employer. These arrangements vary widely in form and function, and careful consideration should be made to examine the delineation of responsibilities in the service agreement.

One likely exception to the concept of a "total administrative outsourcing of liability" is that a 3(16) still needs to be hired by the employer or responsible fiduciary which still has the overriding burden to select, monitor and replace that service provider if necessary. The extent of the liability of selecting and monitoring a 3(16) is subject to some debate and may depend greatly on the nature of the arrangement and the specific language in the contractual agreement.

Few businesses currently utilize a full service 3(16) administrator because of the costs associated with them, but they are slowly becoming more common arrangements. A full service 3(16) will usually take the place of the plan administrator and TPA roles, depending on the scope of services detailed in the agreement.

The Independent Auditor

Independent audits are required for all large plans, generally defined as 100 or more participants. The auditor's responsibility is to form an opinion as to the financial statements and schedules with regards to their consistency and conformity to generally accepted accounting principles. The opinion is made as part of the annual 5500 filing. More information about selecting an independent auditor can be found on the DOL's website at www.dol.gov/ebsa/publications/selectinganauditor.html.

Small plan filers (fewer than 100 participants) are also required to have an independent audit, unless they qualify for a waiver. The specific requirements are found in 29 CFR 2520.104-46; but, in general they must be a small plan and have 95% of plan assets as "qualifying" assets. This waiver must be elected on the 5500 and the Summary Annual Report must be modified in accordance. For more information on the small plan audit waiver, see www.dol.gov/ebsa/faqs/faq_auditwaiver.html.

Independent external auditors must be completely independent of any interest in the result of the audit.

The ERISA Consultant

An ERISA consultant is an individual or entity that specializes in ERISA matters. They can be a Registered Investment Advisor, an attorney or other entity or person so qualified. Consultants assist plan fiduciaries with many different aspects of plan management, depending on the nature of the arrangement and contract.

Consultants can be brought in to consult temporarily on any specific aspect of the plan, but more commonly they serve as long term advisors to the plan. Consultants usually give "plan level" advice and education services to the plan officials and fiduciaries. Sometimes they may offer "participant level" advice, such as education and personalized advice for participants.

Consultants generally operate with a level of independence from service providers and investment companies that allows them to remain unbiased when helping plan sponsors and fiduciaries select, monitor and replace investments and service providers. If the consultant advises the plan on investment matters, they will be a 3(21)(A)(ii) investment advisor or 3(38) investment manager. They can provide many different levels of service, so take time to review their service model and customize it to the needs of the plan.

Securities Brokers

Brokers (also known as agents or advisors, although "advisor" is technically incorrect) are securities licensed and usually insurance licensed producers who are paid by commission or revenue sharing. A broker is NOT an ERISA fiduciary to the extent that they don't trespass into the domain of becoming a functional fiduciary, for which there are specific criteria to meet.

These advisors will generally not acknowledge a fiduciary role to the plan. In fact, brokers are mostly prohibited by their employers from acting in that capacity, and even if they have the capacity to act as a fiduciary (with certain licenses) many financial services firms forbid their advisors from acting as an ERISA fiduciary. Although these advisors can be helpful, they bear little to no liability and generally spend very little time helping the employer with the plan.

Brokers are compensated by commissions and/or revenue sharing arrangements with the other service providers. Often some investments may pay a higher commission or trail to the broker, incentivizing him to recommend it even if it's not in the best interest of the participants. Since he's not a fiduciary he has no liability, but you will if you take his advice without conducting your own due diligence and drawing your own conclusions. There is an inherent conflict of interest for brokers when recommending investments on a platform with variable compensation, but there are some platforms that offer level compensation to reduce the conflict of interest.

Although some brokers may provide educational or enrollment services, in the past they have generally been prohibited by their employers from giving individually tailored investment advice for a participant's 401(k) account. New statutory prohibited transaction exemptions have been implemented under the Pension Protection Act of 2006. In general, the advisor can give individually tailored advice if the advisor receives "level compensation" whereby their advice cannot cause them to receive higher compensation, or by using an approved unbiased computer model. Still, many brokers steer clear of giving individually tailored investment advice for a variety of reasons.

Summary

The two most common problems in identifying the different players in a retirement plan are failing to recognize who may be a fiduciary and differentiating between the roles and responsibilities of the various service providers. Although not all of the service providers listed here will necessarily be associated with any given plan, understanding who is responsible for what is crucial for a fiduciary to evaluate fees for service, a critical fiduciary function. Likewise, knowing the difference between various co-fiduciary service providers will help plan fiduciaries understand exactly what kind and how much responsibility is actually being delegated.

The key understanding for any fiduciary with the responsibility of retaining the services of vendors or co-fiduciaries, is to know that while the appointing fiduciary may be able pass responsibility and therefore liability of various fiduciary functions through the process of appointment, they cannot absolve themselves of the fiduciary responsibility associated with the appointment itself. In other words, if the investment manager you hire fails in his fiduciary duties he will be liable for those failures, but if it can be demonstrated that your appointment for that manager was inappropriate (perhaps because the manager wasn't qualified or had a history of financial negligence/crimes) then the appointing fiduciary can be held liable for a breach of duty in the retention of that co-fiduciary.

For most plan sponsors, if an agent or securities broker was associated with the implementation of the plan, then they are likely being compensated in some way even if they have little or nothing to do with the plan since its installment. Plan fiduciaries should know what that individual is being compensated, and consider replacing an ineffective or absent broker or advisor with an ERISA advisor, provided the advisor can demonstrate the value they can bring to the plan and to its participants and beneficiaries.

CORE ELEMENT 3:
SERVICE PROVIDER RETENTION

THE STORY...

Once upon a time while meeting with potential clients, I came upon a company who probably invited me in only because my conversation with the HR person triggered something she felt she needed to follow up on. During our first meeting I was immediately engaged by her question regarding recent legislative changes, which was something like this: "We heard about this new rule, something about 408, which you mentioned on the phone, but our understanding of that rule is that it doesn't apply to us, correct?"

This was a new situation for me in that the prospect had heard of the rule change, which had just recently been finalized, but had grossly misinterpreted its application. I explained to her, in great detail, exactly what the new rule was and that it applied to every plan sponsor with an ERISA Title I plan. I also explained to her the consequences of failing to follow the rule. She took notes, thanked me for my time, and ushered me out without giving me much of an opportunity to offer my services.

Two days later I received a call from the Chief Financial Officer requesting another meeting as soon as possible. I met him and the rest of the executives the next morning. I was also surprised to be meeting with the company attorney, himself not an expert in ERISA matters. I regurgitated the information I had provided to the HR woman the other day, and found an attentive audience. I also articulated another significant rule change which was going into effect later in the year.

This information caught the members off guard, and I was bombarded with questions about who would provide that information and who had responsibility for this and that, some of which I had no clear answer about since I knew nothing more about the plan than what was available on their plan's 5500 report filing. Annoyed by the apparent lack of communication with their existing plan advisor, I was asked to consult with the fiduciary team going forward.

After communicating with the service providers regarding their assistance with the participant disclosure rule, we instituted policies and procedures whereby the company fiduciaries had a grounded understanding of their duties under the new rules, a formula for compliance, and a thorough documentation process.

✳ ✳

Despite the fact that plan fiduciaries have always had a responsibility to monitor and reduce fees in the interest of participants, for a long time fiduciaries rarely did an effective job because the consequences were not real to them. That time is over. Enforcement by the DOL, new regulations and waves of litigation involving breaches of fiduciary duties related to fees and expenses have now and forever changed the magnitude of responsibility that fiduciaries must adhere to in the interest of self-preservation.

As a fiduciary in today's world, if you fail to understand, monitor and control the expenses that participants pay related to their plan you are inviting attorneys into your business who are chomping at the bit to sue you over your failures. The goals of this section are to:

✓ Expose you to the new fee disclosure requirements and what they mean for fiduciaries;

✓ Explore the prohibited transaction rules associated with those disclosure requirements;

✓ Discuss basic considerations for compliance;

✓ Explore the issues concerning transparency for the purposes of fee analysis;

✓ Demonstrate how different service providers may be compensated;

✓ Review some of the current focal points for regulators and litigators.

The Basic Fiduciary Duty Revisited

As part of the responsible fiduciary's basic duty, a fiduciary has the duty to discharge their duties solely in the interest of plan participants and beneficiaries avoiding conflicts of interest and prohibited transactions, defray unnecessary and unreasonable expenses, select and monitor service providers, act as a prudent man would do in like circumstances, and follow the terms of the plan documents in doing so. When it came to defraying plan expenses, the legislation provides little insight into exactly how that is done. Therefore most plan fiduciaries have had to rely on advisory opinions from the DOL, industry best practices and relevant case law.

The problem of controlling fees and expenses does not rest solely on the shoulders of the plan fiduciaries. For years, service providers have failed to provide adequate disclosures of fees and expenses charged against the plan or how these fees were divided among themselves. Finally after years of deliberation, industry commentary and legal precedence, the DOL took affirmative action and instituted new fee disclosure rules designed to help plan sponsors with improved transparency regarding the fees charged to the plan by its vendors. The success of these efforts has yet to be determined, but if anything they have placed a heavier burden on the plan fiduciaries while only somewhat improving the visibility of fee structures in the contracts they are engaged in.

A Brave New World: 408(b)2 Service Provider Fee Disclosures

The new service provider fee disclosures took effect in the summer of 2012. This rule requires "covered" service providers to give plan sponsors a written breakdown on the expenses charged to the plan annually, and also prior to entering into any contract after the law's effective date of July 1st, 2012.[39] Different service providers may be required to disclose different things depending on the nature of the services provided. For instance, an investment advisor's disclosure would not look the same as a record keeper's disclosure. However in general, all forms of direct and indirect compensation must be disclosed, as well as relevant information for the responsible fiduciary to determine if potential conflicts of interest exist.

The problem with the disclosure rule is that there is no uniform standard for how those disclosures should be made. For instance, one record keeper may issue a fee disclosure statement compliant with the rules that is five pages long, whereas another record keeper, providing principally the same services, may issue a fee disclosure statement that is 25 pages long.

The DOL has issued some guidance on this issue, but to date even with the new fee disclosure rules plan fiduciaries will often find themselves confused or at worst completely in the dark about what they need to know to make decisions in accordance with their responsibilities as an ERISA fiduciary. And because they don't completely understand the disclosures, they often don't even realize how in the dark they really are.

---

39 Employee Benefits Security Administration. (2012). *Final Regulation Relating to Service Provider Disclosures Under Section 408(b)(2).* Retrieved from United States Department of Labor: www.dol.gov/ebsa/newsroom/fs408b2finalreg.html

TRAP #15

NOT COMPLYING WITH SERVICE PROVIDER RETENTION DUTIES UNDER 408(b) 2

New rules implemented in 2012 clarified fiduciary responsibility for plan sponsors when it comes to retaining the services of providers paid by the plan. Many plan sponsors are uninformed about what these new regulations demand or how to comply with them. Failing to comply with the new rules is a prohibited transaction.

Fiduciary Responsibilities under 408(b)2

It is a prohibited transaction to pay a service provider *any fees or expenses from the plan*. Let's go over that again: it is against the law for you to hire anyone to assist with any aspect of the plan and pay them from the assets of the plan! This is another one of our famous "blanket prohibitions" that comes with exemptions. The exemption in this case is compliance with 408(b)2 . Fail to comply with this rule and you have committed a prohibited transaction and subjected yourself to personal liability.

Plan fiduciaries have a responsibility to see to it that they receive these disclosures from their service providers in a timely fashion in accordance with the regulations. Fiduciaries also have a responsibility to request clarification from service providers or consult experts to assist with dissecting a disclosure statement. If a service provider fails to provide the required disclosures within 90 days of request from the plan sponsor, the plan sponsor must report them to the DOL. If the required disclosures were regarding future compensation, the relationship *must be terminated*.

Once the disclosures have been received, the fiduciary must make three determinations in order for the exemption to apply:

1. The services must be necessary.

2. The contract or arrangement must be reasonable.

3. The fees/expenses must be reasonable.

"Reasonableness" is determined by the facts and circumstances particular to each plan, and we will see later, certain steps should be included to determine the reasonableness of services, contracts and fees on an ongoing basis.

Proper prudence in regards to the selection and monitoring of service providers is complex at best. I could write an entire book on the processes and procedures prescribed by law and regulation, opined by the regulatory agencies, best practices of the industry and insights of other industry experts. As I have stated before regarding other areas of plan management, if you are not an expert in understanding, dissecting, and consolidating service provider contracts, you should first consider whether you should seek the assistance from someone with the time and experience to guide you through the process.

Determining What Services Are Necessary

Aside from seeking outside assistance, the first step is to determine what services are necessary for the plan's operation and what services may provide ancillary benefits for the participants and beneficiaries. In doing this you should be able to create a profile of what services the plan will need to seek from outside vendors. As part of this step, you need to consider what services may be paid from plan assets versus "settlor" services. Settlor functions were touched on in Core Element Two "Fiduciary Controls", but for a more detailed reading into settlor functions you should consult the DOL's Field Assistance Bulletin FAB 2003-3 and the Advisory Opinion 2001-01A.

Once you have built a profile of vendor services, you should begin by making inquiries into various vendors to determine who may fit the profile. In some cases the profile may need to be adjusted to take into consideration the current environment of services offered. This is the time to determine what specific vendors may fit the profile and ask specific questions from them. The questions to ask are not only based on what the plan needs, but also to determine their qualifications, experience, business practices, continuity/disaster plans, financial conditions, quality of service and conflicts of interest. You should also consider various arrangements, such as bundled vs. unbundled or open architecture record keepers versus NAV or group annuity providers.

When you have narrowed down the selection, the time has come to get real detailed information based on the demographics and projections for the plan. This usually involves a process known as an RFP, or Request for Proposal. Unless you are utilizing the services of an expert, you will have to construct your own RFP process (something I strongly recommend against unless you are intimately familiar with the process to begin with). Read their responses, ask questions if you don't understand something, and get contract specifics to determine exactly what the service provider will do and what you will be responsible for. I *cannot overstate* how important it is for you to delineate responsibilities between the plan officials and the service providers; many plans have failed fiduciary processes and committed prohibited transactions because they did not understand who was responsible for what.

Once you've evaluated each independent proposal on its own, you'll need to consolidate the data so you can make accurate comparisons between the proposals. This is where a fundamental understanding of the nature of fees and expenses is critical, because even with the new fee disclosure rules it is often very difficult to accurately consolidate information. Part of the reason for this is that it sometimes it will seem too easy to do just that, but the devil is in the details, the financial notes, and the small print of the proposals. We've seen time and again plan sponsors who thought their expenses were X, and after evaluating the proposal/contract in detail we've found they completely misunderstood critical elements of the expense proposals, and often found the plan was paying far more than they realized.

When the consolidation is finished and accurate comparisons are made, you will naturally narrow your selection down to finalists. It is at this time you may want to conduct interviews with the finalists. This is particularly helpful because they may engage you very competitively for business, and in some cases (usually when economies of scale are present) negotiation on the final details are often possible. Formulate a decision and create an implementation plan with the winners. And MOST IMPORTANTLY, document everything you have done in the process and retain all records relevant to your decision making process.

Evaluating Contracts for Reasonableness

Evaluating new or existing contracts for reasonableness is the next required fiduciary step following the determination of services necessary to the plan. Contracts must be determined to be reasonable. Carefully separating vendor and plan sponsor responsibilities is a critical area of contract evaluation. Certain exculpatory provisions are expressly prohibited by ERISA and should be carefully evaluated to ensure they are not part of the contract. Any type of co-fiduciary services or fiduciary warranties offered under any contract should also be reviewed.

Of particular note are contracts involving insurance products or annuities. An in depth discussion of the various provisions that may or may not be found in insurance contracts are beyond contemplation for this text, save the fact that fiduciaries must carefully inspect and evaluate each contract to ensure no undue burdens are placed on the plan or its participants with respect to liquidity, surrender charges, market value adjustments, annuitization provisions, living benefits, termination costs, etc. Some of these contracts can impose mobility restrictions that can have serious consequences for participants and hence for the fiduciaries who engage in their services with an insufficient due diligence process.

The process discussed previously, whereby many vendors are evaluated and compared, can go a long way in determining the reasonableness of contracts by comparison of the prevailing vendor contracts. This is where one of many problems in the industry exist: plan sponsors are often engaged by brokers (non-fiduciaries) who recommend a product or service based on the needs of the broker (i.e. commissions and revenue sharing arrangements), not the plan. Currently there is no prohibition in the industry for this practice, due in large part that brokers are not considered fiduciaries unless they "cross the line".

Nevertheless, I have seen too many examples of plan sponsors I have engaged who told me they picked their current service provider because their broker recommended it, without so much as a hint of due diligence in the process. Plan sponsors and fiduciaries who blindly take the hand of such a representative are inviting trouble.

TRAP #16

FAILING TO ANALYZE AND UNDERSTAND EXPENSES CHARGED TO THE PLAN AND/OR PARTICIPANTS

Although new fee disclosure rules were designed to increase transparency, in effect it has illuminated a real lack of understanding by plan officials about how fees are assessed and collected. Plan fiduciaries have a duty to consider fees in determining service provider retention, but in reality they often need help from professionals because, even in light of the new rules, fee analysis is one of the most complex areas of plan governance.

Determining Reasonableness of Expenses

The final required fiduciary process is determining the reasonableness of expenses paid by the plan. Determining the reasonableness of plan expenses is itself a multi-step process:

1. Identify all service providers who are receiving compensation from the plan;

2 Gather information regarding the forms compensation they are receiving and amounts;

3. Conduct a detailed fee analysis;

4. Benchmark the expenses;

5. Evaluate the reasonableness of expenses based on the benchmarking report;

6. Document the process.

Due to the requirements under ERISA 408(b)2, "covered" service providers are required to provide disclosures to plan fiduciaries annually, so identifying these service providers should be relatively straight forward. The service provider disclosures will also contain information regarding the specifics of compensation, so it is important to identify "covered" service providers and take appropriate action if the required disclosures are not made.

Fee analysis is an in depth process, which will be described shortly. Once the fee analysis is completed, plan fiduciaries need to benchmark the fees. There are several ways to do this, but the most common is to either compare statistical data for similarly designed plans with similar demographics or conduct a proposal request from multiple vendors. While the latter is labor intensive, comparing plan data to statistical references can bridge the gap between a formal RFP while still satisfying the fiduciary requirements. Common data points to include are the overall plan assets, number of participants, average account balances and level of service, among others.

With the benchmarking complete, you should have a clear picture of where the plan expenses fall relative to similar plans. You should now begin the somewhat subjective process of determining reasonableness of expenses. Factors to consider include the level of service provided, the quality and performance of those services, and the effect of services on the plan and participants.

ERISA does not require plan sponsors to seek the lowest cost vendors, but if plan expenses benchmark significantly higher than industry peers, extra due diligence should be exercised to determine the expenses are reasonable and necessary. As always, document the process to demonstrate the prudence of your process.

Fee Analysis

The subject of fee analysis is so abhorrently complex that I am torn as to what level of detail to attempt to delve into. Currently even experts can have difficultly deciphering the intricate nature of these arrangements. I may consider a more detailed evaluation in future editions, but for this edition I will limit the discussion to highlight the true nature of the complexity that, without expert assistance, is nearly impossible for plan sponsors to complete with 100% accuracy.

Plan fiduciaries have a duty to discover, interpret, and analyze all compensation from the plan received by all parties no matter how it is received. The basic premise is simple: Who gets paid what by whom, and how and when do they get paid? The reality is anything but simple. On paper, it may seems pretty clear what the vendor is charging. The reality is that the vendor has relationships with dozens or hundreds of other service providers, some of which may receive a portion of the fees paid from the plan. And as the responsible fiduciary, you are obligated to follow the money trail.

This is where things get complicated, because for years the industry practice has been to shield the plan sponsor from the web of commissions, affiliate fees, and every other method of compensation shared by different vendors. The reason these fee sharing arrangements were so shadowy is because it allows service providers to offer "free" services, but in reality they were being compensated by sharing higher internal charges made against the participants. I'll touch more on the "free" services soon enough, but know that even though the new disclosure rules have required certain disclosures to be made, it has not done enough to help unravel the complex system of fee structures associated with retirement plans.

Fee Basics

There are numerous types of fee structures found in retirement plans, and it's important to start with a baseline understanding of different fee structures you may find. For the purposes of this book, I've broken down fee structures into: frequency, assessment, purpose, and payment. Wrap fees are a special type of fee that will also be discussed.

Fee Frequency

Fee frequency is generally of three types: one-time, service based, and on-going. One-time fees are charged once, such as fees related to plan start-up or termination. Service based fees are charged each time a particular service takes place, such as a loan request or document restatement. On-going fees are collected throughout the life of the plan for expenses related to the day to day plan operations, and may be collected daily, quarterly, annually, or by any other method agreed upon.

Fee Assessment

Assessment refers to the method by which fees are determined. The basic fee assessment structures are: itemized, asset based, or hourly. Itemized fees are level fees that are assessed based on a transaction, interval of service time, etc. This is the billing method most people are used to in everyday transactions. Asset based fees charge a fee determined as a percentage of assets under consideration, expressed as a basis point (1 basis point = 0.01%). Asset based charges are very common in the retirement plan industry. Hourly fees, usually associated with TPA or consultants, are fees charged for billable hours of service.

Fee Purpose

Purpose simply relates to what the fees are charged for. There are four general categories of purpose, and some service providers can collect for more than one purpose. The four categories are: administration, investment management, transactional, and advisory.

Administrative fees are associated with the administrative activities of the plan, most commonly associated with TPA and record keeper functions. Investment management fees are associated with the investment management costs at the fund level. Transactional fees are associated with a particular transaction, usually distinguished by plan level transactions and participant level transactions. Finally, advisory fees are associated with costs for a consultant or 3(21)(A)(ii) investment advisory or 3(38) investment management services to the plan.

Fee Payment

This relates to the "who pays" question: the participant, the plan, or the employer. When the employer pays, he is paying the service provider directly, usually from the general accounts of the business. When the plan pays, fees are taken from the trust or ERISA budget accounts (more on these accounts later). When the participant pays, the fees are deducted from their individual accounts only.

Wrap Fees

Wrap fees are generally "multi-inclusive" fees typically found in the smaller plan market on the bundled group annuity insurance platforms. These plans offer their services for a fee designed to make the operating costs effective for the service provider. These wrap fees can be difficult to dissect to understand their form and function, but nevertheless should be. These platforms are often the only ones economically attractive for the micro and small plan markets, and sometimes for start-up plans but again the devil is in the details.

The DOL's Model Disclosure

The DOL in 2008 released their model disclosure form, designed to help fiduciaries break down and analyze fees reports. The model fee disclosure form has 4 schedules, one each for investments, administrative expenses, start-up costs and termination costs. The form is a great starting point for aggregating data. However, the DOL's version has significant drawbacks as well. It makes no attempt to represent average costs over time with changing plan demographics, it does not record transactional costs at the participant level, and the data can be significantly skewed by certain accounts types and even some mutual funds. Therefore its usefulness is limited to only certain applications.

How Non-Fiduciary Service Providers Are Compensated

Non-fiduciary service providers are compensated by a variety of methods that are determined prior to entering into a contractual arrangement. Typically, service providers will charge either as a percentage of assets or a flat dollar fee or a combination. Transactional participant specific services (such as loans, distribution requests, and other services that are requested by an individual participant) are commonly billed directly to the participant who requests those services. Some service providers may also bill by the hour for ancillary services. Let's examine a couple of situations to see the impact on different participants.

Let's suppose a record keeper imposes an asset based charge of 0.25% for its recordkeeping services. Each participant's account will be billed 0.25% of the assets in that account. This can cause participants with higher account balances to pay a larger share of the recordkeeping costs:

Participant	Account Balance	RK Fee (%)	Annual Fee Paid ($)
John	$1,000	0.25%	$2.50
Jane	$10,000	0.25%	$25
Joe	$100,000	0.25%	$250

Now let's assume a record keeper charges a flat $100 annual fee to all participants in the plan. Just as the asset based charge caused higher account balances to pay a greater proportion of the fees, this method tends to cause the opposite effect:

Participant	Account Balance	RK Fee ($)	Annual Fee Paid (%)
John	$1,000	$100	10%
Jane	$10,000	$100	1%
Joe	$100,000	$100	0.1%

As you can see, each of these arrangements presents unique challenges depending on the demographics of the plan. Remember that service providers are often willing to negotiate on these arrangements, and variations of these arrangements are not uncommon. For instance:

• Flat dollar billing step-ups at certain account balance intervals;

• Asset based charge annual caps;

• Combinations of asset based charges and flat dollar billing.

The FREE Service Provider

If you've ever heard the expression, "if it sounds too good to be true, it probably is," or "there's no such thing as a free lunch," then you can read between the lines about free services.

In general, record keepers and other service providers don't take on your business for charitable reasons, but in some cases it may seem so. This practice is still prevalent today and although in itself it is not wrong, you must carefully scrutinize any contract that offers free services (see the following example under revenue sharing).

The premise is to hook in a plan by offering services that are free. Often times these services are related to the plan's administration, such as recordkeeping or TPA services, and almost always part of bundled product solutions. Plan sponsors sometimes get confused about who pays what, and so often the allure of free services is too tempting to decline.

The free service is (*surprise!*) not free at all. These plans usually limit the investment window to certain fund families that have a relationship with the service provider by volume of business, revenue sharing arrangements, proprietary funds, etc. These funds permit fee "revenue sharing" of the funds' expenses back to the service provider to compensate them for free or reduced services, and often times these funds' overall expense ratios are higher than average.

The short story is this: don't be fooled by the lure of free services, they can be competitive but you must do your due diligence to find out where and how those free services providers are actually being compensated. This is not optional for plan fiduciaries; the list of successful claims against fiduciaries for not accurately monitoring fees is expansive and growing daily.

Revenue Sharing

The most common term you'll probably hear associated with the mess of fee analysis is revenue sharing. Revenue sharing is simply the transfer of fees collected to various service providers or salespersons. These fees are almost always derived from the investments in the plan. Revenue sharing usually involves mutual fund loads, commissions, trail commissions (12B-1 fees), and sub-transfer agent fees.

Revenue sharing arises from the fact that there are many different entities at play when it comes to the investment world: transfer agents, custodians, clearing houses, record keepers, brokers, advisors, etc. Some of these individuals are critical to the sales process or ongoing management and need to be compensated for the services that they bring to the table.

If a service provider is not a fiduciary with respect to the plan, then that service provider is currently permitted to receive revenue sharing payments. Since the vast majority of service providers do not act in a fiduciary capacity with respect to the plan, you'll find revenue sharing a very common and expansive industry practice.

Let's use an example where a broker comes in and helps you with some due diligence and eventually finds a better product for you. In all that time he spent with you, never did you pay him for his time or services. But when the transaction goes through (and possibly every year after) that broker may have received not only a commission, but is also probably receiving some type of revenue sharing from for example, the mutual fund expense ratios. Therefore the broker could be incentivized to sell a product that pays him a higher revenue share, and that is a conflict of interest that plan fiduciaries *at least* must be cognizant of.

Revenue sharing is often determined by the share class of the funds on the lineup. Let's examine an oversimplified example. Consider the following hypothetical funds and their corresponding expenses for a retirement plan with $1,500,000 in assets:

Fund Name	Share Class	Annual Total Expense Ratio	Annual Investment Management Expense	Annual Revenue to Service Provider	Annual Revenue to Broker	Annual Service Provider Fee (Billed)
XYZ Fund	R1	1.60	0.40	0.20	1.00	0
XYZ Fund	R2	1.30	0.40	0.20	0.70	0
XYZ Fund	R3	1.00	0.40	0.10	0.50	$1,500/yr
XYZ Fund	R4	0.70	0.40	0.00	0.30	$3,000/yr
XYZ Fund	R5	0.40	0.40	0.00	0.00	$3,000/yr

In this example, if all of the funds are R1 or R2 share class funds, the service provider would be receiving $3,000/year in revenue sharing fees (while the broker would be receiving $10,500 - $15,000/year in revenue sharing fees). If the funds are all R3 share class, then the service provider would be receiving $1,500/year in revenue sharing and $1,500/year in billable fees. Under R4-R5 classes, the service provider would be billing all fees directly. The broker can set his own fees by recommending funds that compensate him at level he thinks he should receive. Additionally, as plan assets grow, the broker's income grows with it regardless of the actual level of service the plan receives from the broker.

Business owners and highly compensated employees often have higher account balances than rank and file employees. As a result, plans with funds that are in certain share classes will often find that the highly compensated employees and owners are paying more than their fair share of the costs. For example, consider the following census:

Employee	Account Balance	Average Account Balance	Average Revenue Sharing Fees (R2)	Annual Fee Paid Per Participant
Owners (1)	$500,000	$500,000	0.90	$4,500
Key Man (1)	$200,000	$200,000	0.90	$1,800
Employee (4)	$400,000	$100,000	0.90	$900
Employee (8)	$400,000	$50,000	0.90	$450

In this example two of the 14 employees, the owner and key man, are paying 47% of the costs (for platform and broker's fees). Whether or not this arrangement is fair is debatable; however the plan sponsor may be able to shift some of the non-deductible expenses (administrative and advisory fees paid via revenue sharing) in such a way as to generate a tax deduction or more effective tax saving strategy by paying the fees directly from the company's general accounts or paying the fees from the assets in trust while moving the funds to the highest share class, and thereby lowest expense ratio, if available. As with anything, be sure that the plan documents allow any payment method under consideration when using plan assets.

Participants can also find themselves paying a disproportionate share of the revenue sharing. Often times, a variety of funds on a plan's investment window may be associated with different revenue sharing arrangements. As in the previous example, let's assume business owner's portion represents $500,000 but this time he invests his assets in R5 share class funds (paying no plan related expenses via revenue sharing) and his employees invest the majority of their $1,000,000 in R1-R4 funds. If, as in this example, the participants (sans the business owner) end up paying the bulk of the platform costs, you may find yourself paying later on when you are on the receiving end of a lawsuit by the participants.

There are platforms that offer "revenue-neutral" arrangements, whereby the revenue sharing funds are spread out in such a way so that everyone is roughly paying the same dollar amount or percentage of assets. These platforms are growing in popularity because of the belief, right or wrong, that the "spreading out" of revenue sharing reduces fiduciary liability by creating an even playing field and de-incentivizing non-fiduciary advisors from making recommendations that would improve their compensation but not be in the best interest of the plan or its participants.

How Fiduciary Service Providers Are Compensated

If the service provider is a fiduciary to the plan (a hired service provider such as a 3(21)(A)(ii) Investment Advisor, not a plan official), they are **not** permitted to keep revenue sharing payments. There are several methods by which a fiduciary may bill a plan, and each has its own unique benefits and drawbacks for both.

Fiduciary advisors will bill either the plan or the plan sponsor. This is usually arranged between the plan sponsor and the advisor prior to entering into an agreement. The benefits of a plan sponsor paying some of the costs related to the plan is that they may find these costs to be a tax deductible business expense (consult your own tax professional to see if this may apply to you). In some cases the advisor may be able to bill the plan directly by collecting their fees through the trust.

When an advisor bills a plan where revenue sharing arrangements already exist (for instance, where the previous advisor was a broker being paid by revenue sharing), the revenue sharing component that is intended to compensate the broker should be diverted into a new account, known as an ERISA spending account, ERISA bucket, or recapture account. This new account can be used to pay for eligible expenses for the fiduciary advisor and/or offset other eligible expenses paid by the plan and its participants. Plan fiduciaries are responsible for these accounts and how and what they are used to pay for. Not all service providers are equipped to offer or manage ERISA spending accounts.

If a fiduciary advisor finds themselves collecting revenue sharing payments, any payments received by a fiduciary to the plan must be refunded to the plan in the recapture account, which then may be used to offset other participant expenses. Any amount remaining in a recapture account can be used to offset other participant expenses, provide additional benefits, but can NEVER be used for the benefit of the plan sponsor. In absence of a recapture account, advisor fees are collected by the trustee as part of their duties.

The fiduciary model of compensation (known as the Frost model) creates great transparency for the plan fiduciaries responsible for hiring the fiduciary service provider because their fees are negotiated and disclosed from the onset without being disguised under revenue sharing arrangements. Fiduciary service providers may bill as a percentage of assets, a flat dollar amount, by the hour, or any combination.

In general, plan level fiduciaries (i.e. company owners or officials) should never influence the plan to pay them for the time or service to the plan. Although some minimal leeway does exist, you run the risk of attracting and retaining the attention of the DOL.

Negotiating with Service Providers

Plan sponsors usually have more leeway in negotiating services and expenses than they often realize. However, certain demographics can limit the plan sponsor's ability to negotiate. High numbers of participants and/or beneficiaries, low account balances, high turnover, large loan balances, compliance failures, and low overall plan assets are examples of demographics that will have a negative impact on a plan sponsor's bargaining position due to how those specific demographics impact the expenses incurred by the service providers themselves.

Recordkeeping costs are largely a factor of participation and are often closely tied to average participant account balances, but the actual driving costs for the service providers' centers more on the number of participants, technological interfaces, and associated support services. Third party administrative costs are typically driven by plan design complexity, compliance and testing issues and the extent of administrative services the TPA is willing to accept (loan calculations, 5500 preparation, etc.).

Investment advisory and investment management services are more closely tied to assets under management than other service offerings, due to the co-fiduciary "risk premium" associated with the increased assets under management. 3(38) investment management services are most commonly compensated as a percentage of assets under management, but 3(21)(A)(ii) investment advisory services more often have either a percentage of asset or a fixed fee, which may include non-fiduciary functions such as consulting as part of the total costs. Even with a fixed fee arrangement, investment advisory services will often incorporate "escalators" in the contract to factor in the risk premiums not captured by the fixed fee.

When services provider fees are collected through revenue sharing arrangements, service providers can end up receiving annual plan "raises" corresponding to growing assets and contributions in the plan that are not necessarily associated with increased value. Plan fiduciaries should consider negotiating with service providers, especially those providing recordkeeping functions and investment advisory services that typically charge based on assets under management, so that plan fiduciaries understand the exact fixed dollar cost of the service to the plan, and ensure the plan is reimbursed from the revenue sharing arrangement when those fees exceed a negotiated fixed dollar fee.

TRAP #17

IMPROPER USE OF ERISA BUDGET ACCOUNT ASSETS

Very careful consideration should be given when deciding whether or not to comingle credits from different sources in a single ERISA budget account. When participant expenses are not paid equally across the board by participants, using credits from certain sources can introduce issues of fairness when credited equally across the board. Likewise, identifying expenses eligible for reimbursement using ERISA account assets is an important fiduciary consideration. ERISA budget account credits should NEVER be used to benefit the employer or reimburse settlor expenses.

ERISA Budget Accounts

An ERISA budget account is a broad term that loosely describes various accounts created within the plan's trust for the purpose of capturing certain reimbursements to the plan by service providers, participants, or the plan sponsor. Although regulatory guidance on these accounts is limited, certain issues should be considered by plan fiduciaries in utilizing these accounts.

Whether these accounts exist depend on the permissibility in the plan documents and the needs of the plan. Plan documents may need to be amended if a budget account is required that is not permitted. Tracking and reporting of account credits and debits should be coordinated with the appropriate service providers.

The assets of these accounts should only be used to offset plan related expenses or distributed to plan participants. Also, it generally considered bad practice to allow budget account balances to carry over into a new plan year, so fiduciaries should take steps to ensure that assets in the accounts are distributed by the end of the plan year.

Two of most commonly utilized ERISA accounts are the "forfeiture" and "recapture" accounts. Forfeiture accounts typically contain assets disgorged from beneficiaries who terminated their employment during the vesting period and were required to reimburse unvested portions back to the plan. Use of forfeited assets for expenses to be shared equally by participants is a typical use of forfeited account assets.

Recapture accounts are created to capture revenue sharing payments to service providers that are in excess of actually determined plan costs. The excess revenue sharing payments are credited to the recapture account and then often used to offset plan or participant expenses. Recapture accounts are increasingly more favorable to use rather than allowing the service providers to keep the excess payments in lieu of "credits" that can be applied later, because of the strict accounting requirements and the potential for lost credits when a plan changes service providers.

Hidden Costs

Even when you can decipher the cryptic codes and mazes of revenue sharing arrangements, you will still encounter hidden costs that are difficult to determine. These include things such as soft dollar arrangements, float, and affiliate revenue to name a few.

Fiduciaries have to figure out how to make them "unhidden" as much as possible, examine their impact on the plan, and decide on the relevance of these hidden fees. Since most of the revenue sharing and some hidden fees come from the expenses related to the investment funds, a prospectus is an excellent resource for information. Yet even a prospectus can give incomplete information or information that can be confusing.

Fiduciary's Reliance on Proposal Data

Fiduciaries should be careful in their reliance on proposed fees. The methods of fee calculations generally do not anticipate aggregate variables that are affected over time, instead relying on a snapshot fee calculation.[40] You can request this information and use it to construct a more complicated fee analysis, and in some cases that would be the most prudent approach. Nevertheless the fiduciary has the duty to discover, interpret and analyze the data, and failing to do so is imprudent and likely a prohibited transaction.

TRAP #18

FAILING TO ACTIVELY MONITOR SERVICE PROVIDERS

The days of vendors having long tenures as service providers to plans are coming to an end. Many sponsors have retained the same vendors for years because they don't want to go through the hassle of changing to a new vendor. It is okay to retain a vendor for a long period of time if it's justifiable, but you have to know what to consider, how often, and document the process. Under the new rules, failing to monitor service providers is a fiduciary failure.

---

40 Swisher, P. (2012). *401(k) Fiduciary Governance: An Advisors Guide.* Arlington: ASPPA.

Monitoring Service Providers

Fiduciaries have a responsibility to select and monitor service providers as part of their core duties. As we have just recently seen, monitoring service providers is imperative because the facts and circumstances that justified the contract with that service provider will change over time. So the question becomes twofold: what needs to be done and how often must I do it?

There is little specific guidance to the question of how service providers should be monitored. ERISA and the DOL are vague regarding the substance of monitoring service providers. I would suggest monitoring should be "ongoing and always", but in practical applications this makes little sense so we have to create some set of criteria which provides for regular verifiable due diligence and also allows for continual flags that could provoke inspection or increased due diligence.

A common industry best practice is to benchmark comparable services against one another to determine cost effectiveness and the range of services available with respect to the needs of the plan. In this manner we are able to compare service providers' range of services with the industry average costs given a plan's particular demographics. Remember that ERISA does not demand that fiduciaries find the cheapest product on the market, only that they pay only reasonable and necessary expenses. Determining what satisfies these two criteria requires both a subjective and objective analysis.

Necessary expenses can be considered those necessary to the plan's operation and for the benefit of the participants. Naturally certain services such as ensuring the plan remains tax qualified are important to the plan's operation but provide no perceived benefit to the participant. Other services such as recordkeeping provide both operational support and an interface to the participant such that the participant can generally see the value.

Obviously expenses associated with a plan's operation and functionality are justifiable expenses because they are essential, but so are perks to the participants that are reasonable for their continued use and benefit. Having a good record keeper with up-to-date technology, websites, literature, support, and interface could certainly be seen as a justifiable expense. Even having an advisor or consultant providing education or in some cases individualized advice may be beneficial to the participants (assuming no conflicts of interest of course).

It is important to consider the input and suggestions of the participants as a whole when making decisions regarding the use of plan assets that are not absolutely essential to plan operation but may be reasonable and necessary for the participants. Essential too is the consideration of the use of transactional costs, such as loan processing, Qualified Domestic Relations Orders (QDROs), etc. If participants as a whole are extensively incurring transactional costs it would be prudent to consider the significance of that cost in your analysis and proposal requests.

The benchmarking process is done initially through the RFI/RFP and repeated as a necessary throughout the life of the plan. Due to the fact that this process is labor intensive and potentially costly, it begs the question as to the frequency for a full scale inquiry and benchmarking comparison. Again there is little guidance on this subject, but I would say you must consider the facts and circumstances of each plan. A rule suggested by a prominent legal expert in ERISA matters is a baseline of two years adjusted for circumstances.[41]

Aside from benchmarking, other measures should be employed as well. Fiduciaries should look at whether the stated services are actually being provided, and what the quality of the services is. Because both the plan and participants may benefit from services, fiduciaries should consider participant and beneficiary input with regards to the quality of some services.

Fiduciaries should always examine proposed expenses versus actual expenses. A comparison should be made to proposal and projections versus actual costs charged. This is a critical step in the due diligence

---

41 Wagner, M. (n.d.). Case suggests that RFPs may be necessary to fulfill fiduciary duties. *401(k) Advisor*.

process to determine that the plan is not being overcharged. A good proposal will incorporate various scenarios that allow for the service providers to make expense projections based on certain assumptions related to plan's demographics, market movement, etc. A deviation or unanticipated expense should be thoroughly vetted for source and accuracy, and followed by an investigation into what caused the anomaly.

Fiduciaries should also be wary of certain red flags that might pre-empt a due diligence review. Service providers altering contracts, participant complaints, legal or financial trouble are some of many indicators fiduciaries should always be wary of regarding the ongoing vendor service.

If the responsible fiduciary determines that the service provider's expenses are not necessary and reasonable, or changes in the contract make it unreasonable or services unnecessary, they have an obligation to renegotiate or replace the existing service provider. It is this obligation that creates the need to monitor the service provider on an on-going basis having and a process in place that can yield documentable due diligence that also allows for continual observation without incurring excessive expenses related to the monitoring requirement. Failure to monitor your service providers or failure to document your process is a failure in prudence.

Fee Policy Statements

In light of the new regulatory requirements to monitor service providers and fees, many experts are recommending plans adopt a fee policy statement. In short, a fee policy statement provides an administrative outline or guide with regards to policies and procedures for ensuring compliance with the regulatory requirements. Although they are not specifically required by ERISA, the policies and procedures ARE required, therefore specific written guidance for implementation of such controls should be considered.

Summary

The new changes to fee disclosure regulations were designed to deal with a growing and consistent problem in the industry: lack of fee transparency. As well intentioned as the new legislation is, it has also increased the burden on plan fiduciaries to understand exactly what is being paid by whom and to whom that compensation is being paid. The bottom line: it is a PROHIBITED TRANSACTION for a plan fiduciary to pay a service provider for services with plan assets unless the fiduciary can ensure that the services are necessary, the arrangement is reasonable and the compensation is reasonable.

Many plans file Short Form 5500s, where little in the way of compensation is disclosed to the regulating bodies. This only serves to exacerbate the problem: if plan fiduciaries aren't required to report it, they often assume incorrectly that:

1. They aren't required to know it;

2. They aren't required to demonstrate that knowledge;

3. They aren't required to measure or monitor it for reasonableness.

As we saw in this section with "free" services and hidden costs, this approach can allow an intrepid litigator to enter the picture and create a nightmare for plan fiduciaries, as many of the lawsuits surrounding retirement plans today involve excessive fees paid by the plan and participants.

Although most plan fiduciaries are ill equipped to accurately benchmark and justify compensation to service providers, there are ERISA experts who can provide a tremendous amount of support and assistance to fiduciaries. Advisors that are being compensated by plan assets and NOT providing fee analysis and benchmarking should be re-evaluated as to the reasonableness of their contracts, and plan fiduciaries would be wise to consider replacing these advisors with those willing and capable to provide such a critical service to the plan.

And finally, make sure that policies and procedures are in place to monitor the fees charged to and paid by the plan and its participants. The fiduciary should have these policies written and uniformly described and adhered to.

CORE ELEMENT 4: INVESTMENT MANAGEMENT

THE STORY...

Some time ago I was approached by a veteran financial advisor to help him with his client's plan. Although the advisor was very experienced, he did mostly personal investment and financial planning and seldom took on 401(k) business. His client was the business owner and my colleague had replaced the existing advisor on the plan.

We met at the place of business where I learned that the owner had a long standing 401(k) with the same bundled service provider. He had no complaints about the plan and was not motivated to change providers. When I asked what he was doing to benchmark the plan investments and fees, he informed me that he had not done anything since the existing provider was contracted over seven years ago. Although there were clear oversights in due diligence, I agreed to help him evaluate the plan after informing him about the changes requiring plan sponsors to exercise much more intense due diligence regarding plan expenses.

After analyzing the investment window, it became apparent that the original investment setup consisted of very expensive share classes, which provided a nice stream of income to the original broker but charged the plan participants (including the business owner) fees that were far out of the range of the competition; in fact, his fees benchmarked in the highest ten percent for a plan with the same demographics. The plan's service provider (in this case the record keeper) was also using mostly proprietary funds in the lineup, which limited his diversification but provided a means to offer him the original perceived reduced recordkeeping fee.

I showed the owner how impactful those investment fees are over long periods of time, and provided a number of comparable quotes from other service providers for the plan. Although he could clearly see the plan was paying too much, he was reluctant to change from the current service provider. We contacted the existing service provider and negotiated a surprisingly reasonable reduction in share class related expenses with no significant increase in recordkeeping costs, and additionally were able to open up the investment lineup to a fair selection of funds provided by other fund managers. In the end, the client kept his preferred vendor, reduced his costs to the participants, provided a more diverse investment window, and with our help demonstrated due diligence in the process.

* *

Oversight of plan investments, whether they are options made available for participants or are directly invested by the plan on the participants' behalf, are a core and critical function of plan operations and fiduciary responsibility. This is the most common area where plan sponsors seek out the advice of professional investment advisors, but as we have seen investment management is just one of many core fiduciary responsibilities and plans fiduciaries are remiss in only seeking advice for investment management if they are not absolutely competent in managing all other areas of fiduciary responsibility.

The details of investment management are complex and the purview of investment advisors and managers who spend their lives learning the world of investing. A properly managed investment platform includes analysis of investments options, economic environment, statistics, benchmarking, style, and so on. It would be a disservice to the reader for the author to indulge into a dissertation of the educational requirements and minutiae of detail required to understand proper investment management because volumes of books, journals, academic papers and opinions already exist on the subject and are widely available. There is nothing I can do here to make you an investment expert in one book.

Therefore, in the interest of brevity I will limit my discussion to the broad subjects of investment management that the plan sponsor needs to be aware of. The best advice that I can give you is that if you are not an expert, or do not have individuals already in your company with the expertise and willingness to act in a fiduciary capacity with respect to the plan, then your best option may be to outsource the investment management to experts who have the time, skills, and technology to either advise you on how to manage it or manage it for you. The goals of this section are to:

- ✓ Offer an explanation of ERISA requirements for investment management;

- ✓ Walk through who may be responsible for investment decisions;

- ✓ Discuss applications and uses of Investment Policy and Investment Policy Statements;

- ✓ Review the various typical and atypical investment options, and requisite considerations;

- ✓ Discuss various optional regulatory provisions that can provide some measure of protection for fiduciaries with respect to the investment options available under the plan.

ERISA's Requirements

As with all other fiduciary activities, any action must always consider the core ERISA fiduciary duties. Beyond that, ERISA is very broad in its application of prudence to investments. ERISA generally does not advocate or endorse any particular strategy or investment, but it does advocate that procedural processes and due diligence are adhered to by fiduciaries in making the determination whether any particular investment is appropriate for their plan. But once again, prudence standards are not clearly defined, so there is a lot of room for interpretation.

What is clear is spelled out in section 404(a)(1) under the section "Investment Duties". The investment fiduciary must consider the facts and circumstances that they know, should know, or should have known relevant to any decision as it pertains to the investment portfolio and act accordingly. The fiduciary should determine whether any course of action furthers the purposes of the plan, considering the risk of loss or opportunity for gain, the diversification of the portfolio, the current and anticipated liquidity needs of the plan, and the projected return of the portfolio relative to the funding objectives of the plan.[42] Keep in mind that these are minimum regulatory requirements. As I referenced before a complete analysis of the processes, tools, and techniques for proper investment management are articulated in numerous publications that are widely available if you are so inclined.

Responsible fiduciaries need a prudent process to form investment decisions. An example of a prudent process was given in Core Element Two "Fiduciary Controls", but it should be adopted to fit a model that more appropriately addresses investment considerations. Fiduciaries need to consult experts if they are not themselves capable of understanding, analyzing, or evaluating relevant facts and information.

Their duty is also ongoing; an example of prudence at one time does not necessarily protect the fiduciary from the accusation of not providing ongoing monitoring. A good source of information can be found in the Uniform Prudent Investor Act (UPIA). The Act was designed to provide a guideline for trustee investments in non-ERISA trusts. You should consider the UPIA as a supplemental resource, not superseding

---

42 Wagner, M., Migausky, S., & Blynn, D. (2012). The *ERISA Fiduciary Compliance Guide*. Erlanger: The National Underwriting Company.

or necessarily corresponding to the requirements of ERISA and the regulatory opinions of the DOL.

Obviously larger plans in larger companies with greater resources will have more capabilities with respect to managing investments in-house than sole business owner with a few employees, and in general the DOL understands and to some extent does not expect the management techniques to be the same. However, if a fiduciary doesn't feel they are capable of living up to the requirements of the law, they have duty to consult with or appoint a fiduciary with the expertise and capabilities of doing so.

Who Is Responsible?

Responsibility over the investment window goes back to the trustee assignment mentioned in the Prelude to Core Element Three. The trustee will be responsible for the investment decisions of the trust, whether those investments can be directed by the participants or not. If the trustee is discretionary, then they may appoint a 3(38) ERISA Investment Manager and thereby outsource the investment responsibility with the exception of hiring, monitoring, and replacing the investment manager. The appointment of a 3(38) investment manager represents the highest level of fiduciary outsourcing available for a plan's investments.

Absent a 3(38), the trustee can appoint an investment advisor, or 3(21)(A)(ii) advisor. The advisor is responsible for making investment recommendations consistent with the facts, circumstances, and needs of the plan. The trustee can accept or reject the advice of the advisor; the advisor only provides advice and has no functional control over the investment decisions. In any event, discretionary control remains with the trustee and therefore they retain the most liability.

In cases where no trust exists, such as in the case when the plan's assets are held in separate accounts of an insurance company, the fiduciary responsible for investment decisions should be spelled out in the plan's documents. If not, it will remain with the named fiduciary in the plan's documents. Most insurance company contracts will offer 3(21)(A)(ii) or 3(38) investment outsourcing for a fee. These services are usually provided by a third party not directly associated with the insurance company so as to separate the issue of liability for the carrier. As in all cases, the responsible fiduciary should carefully evaluate the insurance company's fiduciary contract.

TRAP #19

NOT HAVING A WRITTEN INVESTMENT POLICY, OR FAILING TO FOLLOW IT

It is widely considered by the industry that not having an investment policy is a failure of fiduciary responsibility. In most cases, this policy needs to be written. Likewise, having a written policy and failing to adhere to it will provide a competent adversarial attorney with a blueprint for how to sue you.

Investment Policy

ERISA requires that fiduciaries responsible for the plan investments have a policy in place for selecting and monitoring those investments. Each policy should be tailored uniquely to fit the needs and objectives of the plan, while keeping the policies of ERISA fiduciary responsibility at heart. Typically the policy will consider what type of investments will be used or offered, determine a set of rules or standards for selecting and monitoring those investments, and determine what services may be necessary in order to achieve the investment goals of the plan.[43]

A variety of different metrics and methodologies may be used, such as asset allocation and diversifications requirements, liquidity, different aspects of risk, efficient frontier or modern portfolio theory, etc. The

---

43   Reish, F., & Santagate, F. (2003). *401(k) INVESTMENTS: Satisfying ERISA's Fiduciary Rules.* CIMA: Building Profits.

DOL has offered opinions regarding considerations that may be prudent or necessary, but ultimately the process and procedures are left to be determined by the responsible fiduciaries. Because of the complexities involved with investment policies, plan sponsors usually outsource much of this responsibility to an ERISA manager, or at least get guidance from an ERISA advisor.

Investment Policy Statements

Investment Policy Statements (IPS) are simply a written form of the investment policy, drafted to assist the responsible fiduciaries with a written policy regarding investment policy. Depending on the structure, an IPS can either be very broad and general or prescribe detailed procedures and specific analyses and actions. The DOL and the courts have determined that an IPS can be viewed as partly demonstrative of prudence and consistent with the requirements of ERISA. The most recent DOL opinion can be found in interpretive bulletin IB 2008-2.

Although it is permissible and consistent with ERISA to have an IPS, it is also not required. An investment process is required; it just does not specifically need to be written down. Nevertheless, it is considered an industry best practice to draft and implement an IPS, and courts have found fiduciaries liable because their processes were either not documented by an IPS or not followed.

Thus if you have an IPS it is important that you follow it, or you will risk providing an adversary with an outline of how to find fault in your management.[44] However, following the directions of an IPS that is imprudent or inconsistent with ERISA would likewise be improper. And by the same token, simply following an IPS is not a defense against imprudence or failing any other core fiduciary function.

An IPS is usually created with the help of an investment advisor, attorney or both. The decision of how to draft an IPS, what it needs to

---

44   Swisher, P. (2012). *401(k) Fiduciary Governance: An Advisors Guide*. Arlington: ASPPA.

contain, and what it may or may not contain is a function of the facts and circumstances of each individual situation. A fiduciary taking on the investment management responsibility should consider the use of a well drafted IPS and be careful to follow it. Alternatively, one should be careful not to impose rigidity in the decision making process or otherwise expose the fiduciaries to unnecessary liability.

Selecting Plan Investments

Selecting the investments to be used is the first step in the investment management process. Any consideration of an investment or investment option should take into account the investment process already discussed, and knowing a few key fundamentals of retirement plan investment options is important to begin formulating that policy.

Active vs. Passive Investment Strategies

In recent times there has been a focus on whether the fees and expenses associated with active fund management are worth the performance, and what role passive investments may play. Active investment managers are "active" in monitoring, buying, and selling a fund's underlying securities. This activity is usually designed to time the market, take advantage of arbitrage, replace poor performing or risky securities with better ones, or nearly any other strategy imaginable.

Active trading patterns create some inherent issues caused by the strategy. First, expenses are normally higher for actively managed funds because of the numbers of researchers, analysts, and managers that normally comprise the investment management team. Second, with respect to funds invested outside a qualified retirement plan for example, taxes tend to be higher, because short term trading patterns generate short term capital gains and losses. Finally some active managers are inconsistent when it comes it performance, especially during certain market cycles, compared with their index, strategy, benchmark or peers.

Passive investment strategies, or "index" strategies as they are often referred to, involve a management team that selects the underlying fund's investments but otherwise plays a minimal role in trading securities in and out of the portfolio. Passive investment strategies have gained in popularity because of the low expenses associated with that management style. Likewise, passive investments do not benefit from experienced, well performing active fund management teams who may outperform a passive strategy by taking advantage of buying opportunities and arbitrage in the markets.

There are no definitive answers with respect to active versus passive management styles, and in many cases the decision to add a fund strategy to a plan or portfolio may come down to familiarity, preferences, and participant needs.

Standard Plan Investments

The most common investments you'll find in retirement plans are separate accounts (from insurance companies), mutual funds, exchange traded funds, and collective investment funds.

Mutual Funds

Since we've already reviewed separate accounts in Core Element One "Plan Design", we're going to skip right into mutual funds. Mutual funds are simply pools of assets invested in other securities. When someone purchases a mutual fund, they are purchasing "shares" at a specified price. The price of the mutual fund (net asset value or NAV) is recalculated daily based on the fund's underlying investments, and each shareholder participates equally in the gains and losses of the fund. Investment managers operate the fund and buy and sell securities according to the underlying fund's strategy or objectives.

Mutual funds are commonly offered for retirement plans and come in different "share classes". Share classes are associated with how fees are collected from the participant and/or distributed by the fund company to other service providers. R-share classes are most commonly associated with retirement plans. Although much less common, there are still A (front loaded with low 12b-1 fees) and C (no load with high 12b-1 fees) share class mutual funds to be found in retirement plans. 12B-1 fees are fees collected in the funds associated with marketing by the investment provider. Specific information on share classes varies with each fund company, and to date there is no specific standardization for R-share classes so you should consult the prospectus for each fund for a full description.

Mutual funds have the advantages of diversification in large pools of securities, professional investment management, and benefit from pricing models that limit intraday trading strategies since they are priced only once per day. There are also disadvantages associated with fees and commissions, redemption risks, tax inefficiencies, and poor management practices associated with some investment managers. Index funds are passively managed and thus reduce some fees and management risk associated with more active fund management styles.

Exchange Traded Funds (ETF)

Until relatively recently, Exchange Traded Funds (or ETFs) were not commonly found in retirement plans, but that is changing. ETFs are baskets of securities that are assembled generally for the purpose of tracking a specific index or benchmark. ETFs are mostly "passive" investments, meaning the investment management in minimal, meaning little if any buying and selling of the underlying securities. There are some ETFs that have some tactical guidance and therefore may have more active trading of the underlying securities.

ETFs are priced continuously throughout the day allowing them to trade like individual stocks as opposed to mutual funds. ETFs have advantages related to diversification, low fees, intraday trading, and tax efficiencies. ETFs also have disadvantages such as uncorrelated pricing effects, typically lower dividend yields, complex leveraging strategies, and lack of availability on many retirement plan platforms.

Collective Investment Funds (CIF)

Collective investment funds are trusts created and administered by a trust or bank that pools assets together for strategic investment objectives. CIFs are only available in qualified tax-exempt retirement plans.[45] CIFs are similar in many aspects to mutual funds and ETFs. CIFs can be actively or passively managed.

Advantages of CIFs include diversification and low costs and fees due to lower marketing, administrative and compliance costs. Disadvantages of CIFs include transparency issues, regulatory differences, and issues with portability.

TRAP #20

NOT RECOGNIZING INVESTMENT OPTIONS THAT REQUIRE INCREASED DUE DILIGENCE

There are some investments, although not improper in and of themselves, that require increased due diligence. Plan sponsors often incorporate these investment options for various reasons, but being able to identify what investments may require increased due diligence is an important step in determining whether or not they belong in your plan.

Unitized Investment Considerations

Certain assets may be unitized before they can be invested by participants in a retirement plan. Unitization is the process whereby an account is created that represents an undivided interest in a portfolio of assets, called "units" (a process very much similar to insurance separate accounts). These units are priced and tracked in various retirement accounts usually using daily valuation. Unitized investments may

---

45 American Institute of CPAs. (2010). Plan Investments in Bank Collective Investment Funds. *AICPA Employee Benefit Plan Audit Quality Center*.

include CIFs, ETFs, unitized managed accounts (UMAs), employer stock, and other investments.

Fiduciaries need to be aware that unitized investments have certain advantages and disadvantages to them that can warrant somewhat greater scrutiny than your average mutual fund investment.

Self-Directed Brokerage Accounts

Self-directed brokerage accounts are not investments in and of themselves, but rather investment windows which open the participant up to investments not normally available under the plan's investment window. As the name implies, these are brokerage accounts that allow the participant the opportunity to invest in any investment permissible under the custodian, from individual securities to managed accounts.

These accounts have unique challenges that have not been fully tested in the courts. Uncertainty exists about the extent of the fiduciary's liability for the participants' access to any investment and if or how monitoring of those investments is accomplished. Additionally, 404(c) protection (detailed later in the section) may not apply for these kinds of accounts. Currently, the DOL is looking for opinions from industry professionals to possibly revise regulation for self-directed brokerage accounts.

Non-Standard Plan Investments

It is not uncommon to find very odd and often inappropriate investments in retirement plans, mainly because ERISA does not directly prohibit any particular investment and plan sponsors often don't do enough research, get bad advice, or just don't know any better. At a minimum, the two special considerations for unusual investments are straightforward:

- Is there anything about the investment that could violate any of the basic fiduciary duties of exclusive benefit, prudence, loyalty, obedience and diversification?

- Is there anything about the investment or use of the investment that would cause a prohibited transaction? [46]

Naturally, all investments need to be carefully chosen and monitored, but when the investment being considered is outside the normal realm of mutual funds, separate accounts, exchange traded funds, or collective investment funds, then an even more cautious approach should be considered.[47]

Any investments that have characteristics such as more risk, difficult valuation, transparency, reduced diversification, increased expense, liquidity restrictions, redemption fees, or create similar complications should be very carefully evaluated; fiduciaries should consider a legal opinion on the investment in question.

Monitoring Plan Investments

Monitoring plan investments is one of the key policy functions for the fiduciary responsible for the plan's investments. Metrics and methodologies used for monitoring plan investments is left to the fiduciary along with legal framework, regulatory opinions, and industry best practices used as guidance in determining the process and procedures.

Investments should be monitored with regularity. Usually this is done quarterly but not always. If an investment or investment options fails to meet its required criteria to remain in the plan, it should be replaced in accordance with the investment policy.

---

46 Swisher, P. (n.d.). Stupid Investment Tricks: Interesting, Risky, or Downright Dumb Retirement Plan Investments. *Journal of Pension Benefits*.

47 Swisher, P. (n.d.). Stupid Investment Tricks: Interesting, Risky, or Downright Dumb Retirement Plan Investments. *Journal of Pension Benefits*.

TRAP #21

NOT INCORPORATING BASIC STEPS TO REDUCE YOUR LIABILITY FOR PARTICIPANT INVESTMENT DECISIONS

Fortunately, many options exist for plan fiduciaries to limit their liability when it comes to participant investment decisions, and it's amazing how many plans don't take advantage of these options. At the same time, you must comply with the strict requirements for their use; otherwise they are as good as nothing.

Reducing Fiduciary Liability

Plan investment fiduciaries have two major weapons to help reduce their liability: 404(c) protection for participant directed accounts, and qualified default investment alternatives (QDIAs).

Participant Direction and ERISA 404(c)

Plans are designated by the ability of participants to direct the investment decisions of their individual accounts on the form 5500. For plans that permit participant direction, the plan can elect on the form 5500 an acknowledgement that the plan intends to comply with ERISA section 404(c). 404(c) is an optional election, but compliance with it can provide some benefits that plan sponsors often, but incorrectly think they already have. So before I talk about what 404(c) may protect the fiduciaries from, we should first address what liabilities they are already exposed to.

In practice, the application of ERISA says that the responsible fiduciary (whoever is so designated) is responsible for all aspects of investment management. When the plan provides that the responsible fiduciary determines the investment allocation of the participants' contributions where the participant has no influence or control over the investment, it seems logical that the fiduciary should be responsible for the prudence and due diligence associated with that investment, and that is indeed the case.

Counter-intuitively, for plans where participants make their own decisions about their investments the fiduciary is still responsible and liable for investment decisions *made by the participant*. Yes, you just read that right. In plans where you provide the investment options and allow the participants and beneficiaries to direct their own investment allocation, the responsible fiduciary is still liable for the decisions made by the participants. On the surface, this seems an over-reach of legal application and intention. The technical legal questions involved as to why this is the case are beyond the scope of this book, but needless to say compliance with the optional 404(c) requirements provides a form of limited liability for the fiduciary.

Specifically, compliance with 404(c) exempts the plan's responsible fiduciary from liability for the investment allocation decisions made by the participants in certain cases and provided certain conditions are met. In theory, 404(c) does not protect the fiduciary from the investment decisions at the plan level (the options provided to the participants), and the DOL does not consider 404(c) to be a "safe harbor" so to speak.

It's widely considered by attorneys and industry experts that compliance with 404(c) is an all-or-nothing affair; to be protected by the provision you must comply with all aspects of the provision. As to how far this extends has yet to be determined. For instance, if you fail to meet all the requirements with just one participant, does that liability exemption fail to hold only for that participant's investment direction or for the plan as a whole? These questions have not been fully tested in the courts.

What limited case law does exist seems to favor the fiduciary. In several incredibly surprising decisions, courts have been very liberal in the application of 404(c) and the scope of its protection.[48] With that being said, a prudent plan fiduciary should not interpret these decisions to necessarily apply to their specific circumstances, and instead focus on compliance requirements if the protection is desired.

Intending to comply with 404(c) but failing to do so does not leave the responsible fiduciary with any more or less liability than they would have had if they had never intended to comply with the regulation in the first place.

Additionally, some of the disclosure requirements that were once voluntary under 404(c) are now compulsory and part of fiduciary responsibility with the new participant disclosure rules per 404(a). 404(c) compliance is optional, but 404(a) compliance is not. So plan sponsors who have never attempted to take advantage of the protections of 404(c) for whatever reason, should now reconsider in light of the changes in the requirements.

The application of 404(c) can be more complex than it appears on the surface, and plan sponsors and fiduciaries should consult with competent advisors and/or legal counsel as to the specific requirements of 404(c). In practice this is where there is often a disconnect; fiduciaries must understand who is responsible for what when it comes to 404(c) compliance, and many incorrectly assume this burden will fall under a service provider who may assist with certain aspects of 404(c), but ultimately assumes no final authority or liability with respect to that function.

Also commonly misunderstood is the participant education requirements under 404(c) (this is often misunderstood even by advisors). 404(c) has no education requirement per se. Certain information is required to be provided to participants, most of which currently falls under 404(a) as noted before. There may be, and this has yet to be demonstrated in court, an inference of participant level

---

48   Swisher, P. (2012). *401(k) Fiduciary Governance: An Advisors Guide.* Arlington: ASPPA.

education as being prudent; but specifically there is no requirement under 404(c) to provide participant level education.

TRAP #22

NOT PRUDENTLY SELECTING AND MONITORING DEFAULT INVESTMENTS

Default investments are investments that are allocated to contributions when the participant gives no specific instruction for their allocation. Hence, an inherent liability exists for plan fiduciaries when choosing what investments participants default into. Investment options that limit the fiduciary's liability exist, but many plan sponsors don't take advantage of them.

Default Investments and Qualified Default Investment Alternatives

The concept of "default investments" arises from situations called negative elections, where participants with the ability to direct the investments in their accounts fail to do so. The contributions must be placed somewhere, and it is the fiduciary's responsibility to elect a default investment for those accounts.

We already saw how fiduciaries have liability for "positive" elections unless they seek 404(c) protection, but clearly default investments seem to inherently harbor more potential for liability. Surprisingly a large number of participants fail to elect their own investment options, which makes the DOL's concern over the fiduciaries choice of default investment all the more important.

In 2006, the Pension Protection Act (PPA) was enacted by Congress and set into motion a series of new laws for qualified retirement plans. Among them, a safe harbor was provided for default investments, known as Qualified Default Investment Alternatives (QDIA). By using a properly implemented QDIA, a plan's fiduciaries can be absolved from liability for participants' negative elections. QDIAs are optional; plan fiduciaries can choose to retain all the liability if they so choose. Additionally, one does not need to comply with 404(c) to utilize a QDIA and vice versa.

There is a six-part conditional test for implementation of a proper QDIA, which is summarized as follows:

1. The negative election of assets of a participant must be put into a designated QDIA;

2. There must be no participant election otherwise;

3. Certain notices must be provided before becoming eligible, and annually thereafter;

4. Pass through information must be provided to participants at least quarterly;

5. Participants must be allowed to move out of the QDIA at least as frequently as they are otherwise allowed to reallocate their accounts, but no less than quarterly;

6. And the plan offers a broad range of investment options, as per 404(c) and the duty to diversify.[49]

Plan fiduciaries need to be aware that to qualify for liability relief they must comply with all six parts of the test. Plan sponsors often fail in submitting the required notices on time and in regards to the pass through information requirement, which can be difficult to comply with. In some cases this author has seen plan menus designed solely using QDIA products, but by failing to properly diversify the investment options the plan's responsible fiduciary may have not only failed in their duty of diversification but also possibly failed to comply with part six of the QDIA test, thus exposing the fiduciaries to liability.

---

49 Swisher, P. (2012). 401(k) *Fiduciary Governance: An Advisors Guide*. Arlington: ASPPA.

Three basic types of investments are designated acceptable as QDIAs, along with two more under limited circumstances. They are:

1. Target Date Funds: Participants are placed into accounts according to their anticipated retirement date, and as the fund ages the equity/debt positions shift from more aggressive to more conservative allocations.

2. Managed Accounts: Participants are placed into accounts that are are actively managed by an investment management service.

3. Balanced Funds: Participants are placed into accounts with a "balanced" (but not necessarily equal) distribution of equity, debt, and cash consistent with the risk level of the participants in the plan as a whole.

The next two are more limited in their application:

4. Money Market or Liquid Fund: These investments qualify as QDIAs only for the first 120 days after the participant's first investment.

5. Stable Value: Default investments in stable value funds prior to December 24, 2007 will qualify as a QDIA as long as there is no penalty for withdrawal.

An investment advisor can assist the plan's fiduciaries in understanding the rules and application of QDIAs as appropriate to each plan.

Target Date Funds (TDFs)

In practice the most commonly used QDIAs are Target Date Funds (TDFs). TDFs are mostly mutual funds (although some are CIFs or ETFs) designed to slowly de-risk the portfolio over time, at a rate known as a "glide path". Glide paths may be "to" retirement, settling on an asset allocation profile once a certain age is reached, or "through" retirement, continuing to reallocate the portfolio for some period of time after the anticipated retirement age. Glide paths and "to-through" investment styles vary from one company to another.

Investors who default into these funds default according to their age and/or anticipated retirement date. For instance, XYZ 2050 Target Date Fund would allow default investors whose anticipated retirement year is on or near the year 2050.

Due to the vast amounts of deposits going into these funds and their complexity and variation, the DOL is aggressively working on new rules regarding the use of these funds and fiduciaries have a requirement to understand all aspects of these funds upon making a decision to implement them. Therefore, extra caution should be exercised when implementing a target date fund option, due primarily to the increased scrutiny from regulators.

Managed Accounts

Managed accounts are unitized accounts that are managed by investment companies for the individual investor's specific needs and risk tolerances. Managed accounts come in a variety of flavors, such as Unitized Managed Accounts (UMAs) or separately managed accounts (SMAs). Managed accounts may be managed for a specific risk tolerance, or a uniquely managed solution tailored to the individual. Managed accounts may or may not charge an additional participant fee for their services.

Balanced Funds

Balanced funds are usually mutual funds (but sometimes CIFs or ETFs) that are a mix of various asset classes, usually comprised of equity/debt securities such that there is not a significant overweighting of either asset class. Balanced fund QDIAs are chosen for the overall demographics of the plan, not necessarily because of any individual investor's demographics or risk profiles.

Money Markets, Guaranteed Insurance Contracts (GIC), and Stable Value Funds

Money markets, guaranteed insurance contracts, and stable value funds are all cash equivalent investments, usually providing low risk and return, and sometimes good liquidity. As noted earlier, these investments only satisfy as QDIAs under very limited circumstances. These investments have also come under specific scrutiny from regulators, and since each with their own set of advantages and disadvantages they should be carefully weighed before offering them to participants as part of an investment menu.

Summary

Managing the investments in a qualified plan is possibly the most complex area of plan management, and while one can learn the administrative roles fairly easily it would take years of study and insight to properly manage investments. Unfortunately many plan sponsors take on this responsibility without realizing how highly litigated this area really is. This is why I kept this section short; I can't teach you what you need to know to properly manage the investments in one book.

There is a cornucopia of information available on the web if you really want to concern yourself with it, however I find most plan sponsors are busy enough and can't bother with becoming investment experts for the sake of an employee benefit plan. Therefore, if you are not an expert in investment management then I highly recommend you retain the services of someone who is.

If you do decide to retain discretion, then you can limit your liability if you take advantage of certain provisions such as 404(c) and QDIAs. Additionally, a properly drafted IPS can help guide your decision making process. In any event, it would be a good idea to consider retaining an investment advisor to at least provide some guidance on how to properly comply with limited liability provisions/safe harbors, industry best practices and proper investment management implementation.

CORE ELEMENT 5: ADMINISTRATIVE MANAGEMENT

THE STORY...

I was asked to meet with an executive at a local manufacturer at the request of an acquaintance who worked in their human resources department. The company in question had a large retirement plan and was well known in the community. I arrived and soon after met with one of the company's executives and the HR supervisor. The executive seemed to be put off by the whole meeting, possibly because she expected me to come in there and pitch them another plan vendor, a common tactic by brokers but that was the last thing on my mind. The HR supervisor was engaged but seemed rather young for her position.

As I soon found out, the plan had no active advisor and the HR supervisor was the daughter of the owner, seemingly only a few years out of college. Their company had felt a delayed effect on their production after 2008, and was now experiencing a contraction in their sector. Profitability had been poor the previous year, and the executives had made a decision not to match employee contributions but had yet to inform the employees. Apparently this was the reason I was asked by the other individual to come in; only a select few knew about the decision. And to make it more interesting, the decision to withhold the match came at the beginning of the next calendar (and plan) year but retroactive for the previous year.

My acquaintance, who had worked in human resources for over 20 years, had advised the HR supervisor that such a move may cause discord among the employees because a match had already been declared to the employees in writing during the previous plan year. The HR supervisor had agreed to meet with me to seek advice about what they could do regarding the disclosure, or if it was even necessary. I examined the plan document and disclosures already given to the participants, and discovered that the employer had an annual discretionary contribution arrangement, but their subsequent decision may have violated both their own document's directive for timing and participant disclosure rules.

I advised them both that their plan documents did not appear to permit such action, that it was possible that they might be on the hook for the previously disclosed match due to its disclosure to the participants, and that there was a need to ensure that there are no violations of anti-cutback rules. In any event I informed them that they should consult with an ERISA attorney on the matter because I was not qualified to give legal advice, but I could certainly guide them once a clearly marked path of legal compliance was given.

This got the attention of the executive, who in a terse tone, informed me that the company only offered the plan at its discretion, had the right to terminate the plan at any time, and in this case they felt the move was necessary to keep from having to lay off any more employees. I advised her that even though she was correct in her points, they had a duty to obey their own document's directives unless those directives are amended, and the time for discretionary plan amendments had passed for the previous plan year. I left them with some words of wisdom and three business cards for local legal services specializing in ERISA matters, sincerely hoping they would take my advice and seek counsel.

I was contacted many months later by the acquaintance in HR who arranged the meeting with me in the first place. Although I couldn't discuss my conversation with her supervisors, she informed me that the company eventually informed the employees of the move, and it was horribly received. She told me that the company had just recently been contacted by the DOL following up on participant complaints, and based on those conversations the company was in the process of retaining counsel in anticipation of a formal investigation.

Employee complaints are one of the top reasons for DOL investigations, and in this case a little caution and understanding of their own plan documents and disclosure rules could have prevented what is sure to be a time consuming, expensive endeavor.

* *

Administrative management deals with the area of plan governance and operations, with the responsibility generally falling on the plan administrator. I will introduce you to the basics and point out some areas of concern, but the majority of the complex administrative calculations, particularly with regards to testing requirements, should be outsourced to a competent TPA. The goals of the section are to:

- ✓ Differentiate between IRS and DOL requirements;
- ✓ Provide definitions for problematic coverage questions;
- ✓ Highlight important areas of administrative governance that cause common problems;
- ✓ Incorporate new disclosure requirement rules;
- ✓ Review the importance of plan documents;
- ✓ And discuss the various means of recourse for mistakes.

IRS Administrative Requirements

ERISA Title II sets forth amendments to the Internal Revenue Code §401 for specific requirements related to plan compliance. These requirements generally fall under the authority of the IRS. This include coverage, nondiscrimination, vesting, contribution limitations, and taxation of deferrals and withdrawals. Plans must test regularly against the IRC rules, and the testing is a complex endeavor. Again, the majority of these provisions are far too complicated to be explained here. The compliance monitoring of IRC requirements are typically outsourced to a third party administrator (TPA).

TRAP #23

FAILING TO UNDERSTAND AND COMPLY WITH PLAN DOCUMENT REQUIREMENTS

Compliance with the plan document's provisions is a fiduciary function. Unfortunately, fiduciaries sometimes make decisions without regard to permissibility or prohibition by the documents. Plan documents usually can be amended, but violating the document's provisions is a common fiduciary mistake.

The Plan Document

The plan document is the heart of the plan. It determines all the conditions of the plan and sets forth the rules for operation. An administrator MUST follow the plan documents, and do nothing expressly prohibited by the documents or ERISA.

There are certain basic provisions required by ERISA and the IRC that these documents must contain. Therefore, the IRS permits four types of plan documents to be used (note that generally only one of these will be used per plan). The first is the Master/Prototype plan, which consists of an adoption agreement (essentially a checklist of what provisions the plan sponsor decides to implement) and the plan document itself which contains all of the necessary qualification language. This is the simplest, most cost effective way to construct the plan documents but also the least flexible. In general, the M/P plan documents are pre-approved by the IRS except if using a nonstandardized adoption agreement. The nonstandardized adoption agreement in an M/P submission is considered the second type of allowable document, but it must receive an opinion letter from the IRS.

The third type of permissible plan document type is known as the volume submitter. It is considerably more flexible than an M/P plan document but generally more expensive to construct. A volume submitter may need to be submitted to the IRS for an advisory letter. Finally, individually constructed plan documents can be created for complex design and/or testing requirements. These will almost always involve an attorney. They are the most expensive, but most flexible plan documents to use. They will also require a favorable ruling by the IRS.

Aside from the required language, plan documents can allow for many kinds of provisions, which may include but certainly are not limited to:

- The naming of all fiduciaries;
- Roles, functions and limitations of fiduciaries;
- Definitions of compensation;
- Who is responsible for paying certain fees associated with administration;
- The ability to amend the plan document;
- Provisions for loans, in-service withdrawals, and other participant related discretionary options.

It is important to note that plans can be constructed so that their "end of year" corresponds to whatever date the sponsor chooses, but it is typically set to the sponsoring company's fiscal year. So for plans with non-calendar years, certain required actions on dates "from the end of the plan year" will correspond to different dates than calendar year plans.

Plan documents are required to be updated periodically to reflect legislative and/or administrative changes. They are required to be amended every five years for individualized plans or six years for pre-approved plans on a remedial amendment cycle that corresponds to the last digits of an employer's EIN. Additionally, interim amendments may be required between those five and six year cycles, depending on legislative changes. *In a recent webinar the IRS claimed that failures to amend plan documents continue to be the largest issue in the industry from their perspective, so careful coordination with your TPA and other service providers should be followed to ensure compliance with IRS regulations.*

The TPA Function

Enter the third party administrator, or TPA. A good TPA is an expert in plan compliance with the IRC. A typical TPA consists of various people with expertise in plan administration and compliance. The function of a TPA cannot be overstated. Contracting with the wrong TPA can be disastrous to a plan because so much of their work will determine whether the plan remains tax qualified. A plan determined by the IRS to be unqualified will have negative tax consequences for everyone associated with the plan, including fiduciaries and participants.

Internal controls, credentials, experience, and reputation in the industry are key to assessing the right TPA for your plan. TPA services vary widely, but in general all will handle the vast majority of the compliance testing for the plan. Some may provide assistance with plan design, participant disclosures, assistance with audits, and other services.

TPA personnel are generally credentialed through the American Society of Pension Professionals and Actuaries (ASPPA). Credentials for pension professionals include, in order of complexity, the Qualified 401(k) Administrator (QKA), the Qualified Pension Administrator (QPA), and the Certified Pension Consultant (CPC). Plan sponsors can inspect the SAS 70 Type II report for a TPA before contracting with them, as the SAS 70 II provides you with an independent auditor's assessment of the TPA's controls and processes.

As I've stated before, the complexity of the testing requirements managed by TPAs' is far beyond the scope of this book, but you need to understand how important the role of the TPA is to proper plan management.

TRAP #24

FAILING BASIC ADMINISTRATIVE DUTIES RELATED TO EMPLOYEE GROUPS, ELIGIBILITY, PARTICIPATION, VESTING AND REPORTING

These failures are more common than they should be, because alliances with good TPAs or bundled service providers providing competent administrative services should minimize the risk to the plan for failing these basic functions. And even with a good TPA, failures can still result when inaccurate information from the business is delivered to the service provider who is tasked with helping the business manage these responsibilities.

Highly Compensated and Key Employees

A key to determining certain types of contribution testing limits is the identification of Highly Compensated Employees (HCEs) and key employees. The job of determining who is an HCE or key employee is generally a TPA function.

An HCE is defined by IRC 414(q) 1 as:

- A person with more than 5% ownership in the business during the plan year or prior year ;

- OR received compensation during the look-back year in excess of the annual threshold (for plan year 2014, $115,000 in compensation during 2013).

HCEs in a plan must be tested for compliance purposes against the non-HCEs in three major areas: participation, salary deferrals, and matching and after-tax contributions. In general, HCE contributions will be limited when non-HCEs are not maximizing contributions. Therefore there is an incentive for business owners and highly compensated employees to get the rank and file employees to participate and contribute to the plan.

A key person is defined by IRC 416(I) (1) (A) as:

- A person with more than 5% ownership in the business during the plan year;
- OR an officer with annual compensation greater than the threshold amount (currently $165,000);
- OR a person with less than 5% ownership but at least 1% ownership and compensation of $115,000 or more.

Key persons are subject to the Top Heavy test, which compares the percentage of assets owned by key persons vs. non-key persons. If the plan is determined to be top heavy, the plan sponsor could be subject to additional minimum contributions for non-key employees and may be subject to minimum vesting schedules.

During my time advising plans, I came across several salespersons for vendors selling service products who put their clients in precarious positions because they would ask the plan sponsor, "Who are your highly compensated or key employees?" without defining what that meant or how to determine it, with the end result being a failure of nondiscrimination or top heavy testing due to ignorance by the salesperson and poor oversight by the (typically) bundled TPA. If someone asks you this question, find another service provider who will help make that determination with you.

Eligibility, Participation and Vesting

Eligibility, participation and vesting schedules are determined by the plan sponsor at plan inception, within IRS guidelines. Eligibility and vesting schedules can also be changed later down the road by amending necessary plan documents, but one should be cautious not to violate IRS anti-cutback rules, which deals with restricting employees accrued benefits.

Once the groundwork is laid for the structure of the plan, the day to day calculation of eligibility, participation and vesting is usually outsourced to a TPA. The business must timely and accurately report census information to service providers responsible for administrative issues with respect to eligibility and vesting. Inaccurate information from businesses is a common source of administrative headaches for both the business and their service providers.

Managing Contributions

Employee contributions are made in the form of payroll deductions. According to the IRS and the DOL, inconsistent definitions of compensation resulting in ineligible contributions or deficient contributions AND failures to timely deposit contributions continue to be a major source of violations. Work with your TPA, payroll service provider, CPA, and any other advisors to ensure the definitions of compensation are consistent between payroll and the plan, and coded appropriately for remittance.

Since 1996 the DOL has required companies to deposit contributions into the trust at earliest day it can be "reasonably segregated" from the general assets of the employer but NO LATER than the 15th business day of the month following the month which the contributions were withheld from pay. THIS WAS NOT A SAFE HARBOR, and many plan sponsors found out the hard way when the DOL audited them and found they had engaged in a prohibited transaction even when they made deposits prior to the DOL dates. For large plans with over 100 participants, this rule remains in effect.

In 2010, the DOL released an administrative "safe harbor" contribution timeline for small plans with less than 100 participants. The ruling states that a contribution will be considered to have satisfied the 1996 requirement if the contributions are deposited in trust no later than seven business days of being withheld from pay or received by the employer (if not automatically withheld).

How to Deal With Mistakes Before They Deal With You

The department of the IRS that deals with correcting plan errors is the Employee Plans Compliance Resolution System, or EPCRS. There are three types of failures correctable under the IRS programs: operational failures, plan document failures, and demographics failures. Additionally, there are three levels of managing mistakes in the plan available through EPCRS: the self-correction program (SCP), the voluntary correction program (VCP), and finally the audit closing agreement program (Audit CAP). I'll discuss briefly the differences between them, but you should consult a professional for your unique situation. For more information, visit the IRS website at www.irs.gov/Retirement-Plans/Correcting-Plan-Errors.

The first step is to determine what type of failure took place, the extent of the failure, and whether policies and procedures were in place to prevent the mistake in the first place. The next step is to determine what correction program is available to you. The self-correction program (SCP) is the easiest to perform and should be the first place to look before correcting errors; however, the SCP only permits correction for operational failures that were not egregious and policies and procedures were already demonstrably in place to prevent such failures, even if they didn't. The voluntary correction program (VCP) is provided for all other failures or operational failures not correctable under SCP.

An Audit CAP is a non-voluntary correction precipitated by an IRS audit. It is the least desirable correction method and may result in penalties and/or taxes even upon correction. It's important to identify errors and correct them, if possible, in advance of an audit. Once a plan has been notified of an audit, any voluntary correction method will not apply. The IRS intends to publish a plan Questionnaire Self Audit Tool (QSAT) to assist plan sponsors in identifying potential problems and procedural issues. To date this tool has not been released; however you can find other resources for compliance checklists on the IRS website.

Care should be taken to evaluate whether or not a prohibited transaction has occurred in the course of other errors. If so, you may need to seek remedy through both the IRS and the DOL. In any event, consult the advice of a legal and/or tax professional to help you determine the best course of action. There is a certain designation known as the Enrolled Retirement Plan Agent (ERPA) which is authorized by the Department of the Treasury to represent a plan before the IRS for a variety of reasons, but many other professionals with the proper background, credentials and experience should be able to assist you with correcting plan errors under these programs.

DOL Administrative Requirements

The DOL administrative requirements are set forth in ERISA, primarily in Title I. There is a considerable amount of overlap between the IRS and DOL, but generally speaking they enforce different areas of plan governance. The DOL is responsible for oversight of fiduciaries, reporting and disclosures. We'll touch on mainly the reporting and disclosure requirements as it pertains to plan administration.

TRAP #25

FAILING TO TIMELY FILE A 5500 AND CATCHING AND CORRECTING ERRORS ON THE 5500

Failing to file the 5500 on time and inaccurate reporting is still commonplace even with extensions available and third party assistance. Filing beyond the deadline requires admission into the Delinquent Filer Voluntary Correction Program, and errors on the 5500 when detected will almost certainly bring the attention of the IRS, DOL, or both.

Reporting Requirements

The plan administrator is responsible for reporting the plan's compliance to the three regulating agencies: the DOL, IRS and PBGC. Fortunately, one set of forms satisfies disclosure to all those agencies: the 5500. There are three main 5500 forms:

- The 5500-EZ, for certain "micro" plans;

- The 5500-SF or "short form", a greatly abridged version of the long form for certain qualifying small plans;

- The long form 5500 with schedules, for large plans and anyone who didn't qualify for the first two.

- Note that there are special rules for counting "participants" in plans with 80-120 participants; refer to the links below.

The 5500 is electronically filed using the EFAST2 system; electronic filing is now mandatory. Most 5500's are prepared by a contracted service provider, but it is the plan administrator's fiduciary responsibility to ensure that the information on the 5500 is correct. Amended reports may be filed if information is incorrectly reported. 5500 filings are required to be submitted within 210 days from the "end of the plan year". So for a calendar year plan, that would be the end of July unless extensions are filed.

An important thing to understand is that a 5500 is a tool that is most useful to an auditor. Therefore you should pay close attention to it, especially the section on "Compliance Questions", fees paid to service providers, certain deemed corrected distributions. For more information about filing the 5500, see www.dol.gov/ebsa/5500main.html and www.irs.gov/Retirement-Plans/Form-5500-Corner.

Additionally, plans are required to file reports for plans being terminated. The subject of termination can be complex and unfortunately continues to be problematic industry wide, but for the purposes of reporting, know that the "final" plan report for a terminated plan should only be made when all assets are distributed from the plan, not before.

In the course of our work with retirement plans we frequently find individuals at a company signing the Form 5500 as the plan administrator that are not the actually the named administrator in the plan documents. This is usually a back office employee who signs the 5500 on behalf of the named administrator out of convenience and otherwise has no other role with respect to the plan. This is most commonly found in professional corporations, frequently in small doctor/dental practices.

This is a clear failure of prudence since it is the plan administrator's responsibility to verify the accuracy of the 5500, and care should be taken to ensure that the person with the responsibility of verifying the accuracy of the information is actually the individual acknowledging that duty by signing the 5500. Additionally, most legal experts believe the person who signs the 5500 is technically acknowledging a fiduciary role in the plan and may be exposing themselves to liability they never intended to accept.

TRAP #26

FAILING TO DISTRIBUTE TIMELY DISCLOSURES TO PARTICIPANTS

This is one of the most common administrative failures, but also easily managed. Certain disclosures must be distributed to participants by certain deadlines or by demand and failure to do so can create tensions between plan officials and participants, not to mention failing to follow the fiduciary duty to disclose information within the regulatory requirements.

Disclosure Requirements

The plan administrator is also responsible for disclosing information about the plan to its participants and beneficiaries. I'm going to get into more detail here, because the rules are often misunderstood if known at all. The administrator has a fiduciary duty to ensure accurate disclosures, and the reliance on service provider construction and verity should never be estimated; it should be verified.

Disclosure requirements are found in ERISA §101. There are four main disclosures required to participants (the fourth will be covered separately): first three are the Summary Plan Description (SPD), the Statement of Material Modifications (SMM) and the Summary Annual Report (SAR).

There are some common denominating requirements that are common sense: minimum content requirements, clearly written, not misleading, no deemphasizing restrictions (hiding in the small print), etc. But there are some distinct differences that you should be aware of, especially when it concerns how these disclosures are received by the participants.

The SPD is the main source of information about plan benefits, rights, and restrictions for the participant. It's essentially a version of the plan documents with the most important information pertaining to the participants and beneficiaries. Different SPDs may be created for different groups of employees with different benefits. SPDs must be given to the participant within 90 days of participation, and beneficiaries within 90 days after first receiving benefits.

SPDs given to participants or beneficiaries must include any Statements of Material Modification (SMM) not already written into the SPD. Periodically SPDs will need to be updated and distributed to incorporate the SMMs. If an SMM is issued during a plan year, you have five years for the SPD to be updated and distributed within 210 days after the plan's year end in that fifth year, including all other modification made during that time. If there are no modifications, an SPD must still be updated and distributed every ten years within 210 days after the plan's year end in that tenth year. For a literal reading of the requirement, see ERISA §104(B).

The SMM is a notice of modification of the plan provided to participants and beneficiaries. The SMM basically allows the administrator to provide an "update" on changes to the plan without immediately creating a new SPD. Administrators must provide the SMM within 210 days of the end of the plan year in which the modification was implemented. The SMM must be provided with any SPDs distributed.

A SAR is essentially a summary of the 5500. It is provided annually within 9 months of the end of the plan year, or within two months of an extension deadline.

Terminated employees disclosures have special disclosure rules for SPDs and SMMs that can be found under DOL Reg. §2520.104B-4.

Blackout Notices

The Sarbanes-Oxley act created blackout notifications as a recent addition to the disclosure requirements for administrators, and they are dealt with separately here because of their attention given on the 5500. A blackout occurs when the participants/beneficiaries are limited or prohibited from directing/diversifying their assets or obtaining distributions or loans. If the period of restriction is three consecutive business days or less, no blackout is considered to have occurred and no disclosures are required.

For blackouts beyond three consecutive business days, an advance notice to participants is required. The notice generally needs to be distributed between 30 and 60 days in advance of the blackout; however it can be shorter than 30 days if the administrator certifies, in writing, to events occurring beyond their control or foresight. Specific best practices will apply to handling late disclosures, and specific exemptions for the minimum 30 day rule include:

- Any reason that would violate the exclusive benefit or prudent man rules;
- An event that was unforeseeable or beyond the reasonable control of the administrator;
- The blackout is the result of a corporate merger, acquisition, or similar action.

If any changes occur to the blackout period, notification should be given to the participants as soon as possible. Failure to properly distribute blackout notices is reportable on the 5500.

Foreign Language Requirements

Plans with certain numbers of non-English speakers (not bilingual) are subject to separate rules governing the SPD, SMM, SAR, and presumably blackout notices. Essentially, qualifying plans must provide instructions for obtaining assistance in their language. For small plans (under 100 participants), 25% or more participants literate in the same non-English language qualify for the requirement. For large plans, there is a two part test:

- 500 or more participants literate in the same non-English language, or

- 10% of the participants literate in the same non-English language.

Separate groups speaking separate languages that qualify under these rules must be given instructions in each of their respective languages.

Additionally, the IRS has indicated a growing problem for plans that have participants with invalid social security numbers. According to a recent IRS webinar, currently approximately 1 out of 7 social security numbers are associated with more than one name...that is over 40,000,0000 social security numbers!

Invalid social security numbers can cause violations of ERISA's participation and non-discrimination rules, which will create headaches for plan sponsors and fiduciaries. The IRS recommends using the Social Security Verification Service to help employers identify and correct problematic social security numbers. The verification service can be found at www.ssa.gov/employer/ssnv.htm.

Distribution Rules

One of the most critical responsibilities of the administrator is to ensure that participants and beneficiaries receive the information required in a manner that is appropriate and consistent with the law. To that end, administrators are responsible for distributing this information in a manner that should reasonably ensure receipt by the intended party. Administrators are also required to furnish certain information requested by a participant or beneficiary within ten calendar days of requesting it.

Hand delivery to all participants and beneficiaries would be an appropriate, although often impossible method of delivery. As such, mailing by first class mail is acceptable. Second or third class mail is acceptable only if return and forwarding postage is guaranteed, address correction is requested, and any returns are resent using first class mail or personally delivered. Additionally, providing these disclosures in company periodicals is acceptable if the distribution list is up to date containing all participants and beneficiaries, and a notice is placed on the first page of the periodical advising readers that important plan related information is contained and should be retained.

NOTE: According to DOL Reg. Section 2520.104b-1(b) (1), "....in **no case is it acceptable merely to place copies of the material in a location frequented by participants..."**

Due to the efficiencies and low cost of electronic distribution, new rules have been instituted for electronic delivery. It is acceptable to provide electronic disclosures provided the system ensures actual receipt and confidential information is protected. Participants must have regular electronic access at the workplace as part of their duties, or else consent in writing to electronic delivery. In any event, a participant can always request the paper version.

The New Participant Disclosure Rules

In 2012, new disclosure rules went into effect relating to plan expenses paid by the participants, known in the industry as the 404(a)5 participant fee disclosure rule. It is the plan administrator's responsibility to ensure the disclosures are given properly to participants. However there is a reasonable allowance for accuracy assumed by the administrator for disclosures provided by the service provider, as long as a good faith arrangement exists. Fees charged against participant accounts must be disclosed quarterly, with a more detailed disclosure made annually.

This rule requires disclosures on general plan related information, plan expenses and fees, participant expenses and fees, and greater investment disclosures. The goal of the rule is to provide greater disclosure to the participants regarding the rights when investments are self-directed (controlled by the participant), greater fee transparency, and better information about investment options available in the plan. Even though many service providers (such as record keepers and/or TPAs) will be assisting plan sponsors by providing these disclosures, due to the complexity of the new rules guidance by an advisor with knowledge in this area is highly recommended.

TRAP #27

FAILING TO CORRECT ADMINISTRATIVE ERRORS

When errors are made, corrective processes are usually available to correct them (except in the most egregious circumstances). Plan sponsors often allow administrative errors to go on without correction or reporting, thereby greatly increasing their liability. Fortunately fairly straightforward processes exist for correcting administrative errors; however the regulating agencies will not take kindly to administrators who attempt to cover up their failures.

Dealing with Prohibited Transactions: DFVCP and VFCP

The Department of Labor offers two programs for correcting prohibited transactions: The Delinquent Flier Voluntary Correction Program (DFVCP) and the Voluntary Fiduciary Correction Program (VFCP). As the name indicates, they are both "voluntary" in the sense that the plan officials must initiate the process by applying to the DOL to use the program; if the DOL notifies the plan of an audit and uncovers errors, these options are generally no longer available. Unlike the IRS's self-correction program, these programs do not technically permit "self-correction".

The DFVCP is a program specifically for plans that fail to submit their 5500 by the deadline or extension, if the latter was requested. Civil penalties may be reduced if the filing is made prior to notification of late filing by the DOL. If such a notice is received by the IRS or DOL, you may still be eligible to file under DFVCP rules. A notice from the DOL of its intent to assess a penalty is disqualifying for participation under DFVCP.

The VFCP, as mentioned earlier, is the place to go for correcting fiduciary violations. Submission to VFCP may allow for the fiduciary to avoid the IRS excise tax penalty, if it is applicable. DOL penalties may still apply. VFCP lists a number of "applicable" violations for filing under the program. Full and accurate disclosure and correction are required, or else the application will be rejected which will usually result in enforcement action. Be careful to document everything carefully, because careless documentation will almost always result in enforcement action by EBSA (the enforcement arm of the DOL for benefit plans).

As always, consult with a legal or tax professional if you uncover an error. More information about DFVCP can be found at www.dol.gov/ebsa/newsroom/0302fact_sheet.html. More information about VFCP can be found at www.dol.gov/ebsa/newsroom/fs2006vfcp.html.

Dealing with Regulatory Audits

One of the most intimidating issues for plan sponsors is dealing with the dreaded DOL or IRS audits, but in reality, these investigations can be properly mitigated with good planning, preparation and with the assistance of a knowledgeable consultant and ERISA attorney. It is good practice to anticipate an audit at any time because the regulating agencies not only investigate plans that are suspect (based on employee complaints or 5500 disclosures), but may also instigate random audits based on their enforcement projects.

Prior to any investigation, plan fiduciaries should make sure everything is internally documented in an orderly fashion that corresponds to what the agency may expect the documentation to reflect. When an audit is triggered, it is important to understand what will happen, in what sequence and what will be expected of you. More specific information about IRS audits can be found at www.irs.gov/Retirement-Plans/EP-Examination-Process-Guide.

Regardless of whether the initial communication is simply a request for information or a notification of an investigation, failing to respond to an inquiry will almost certainly escalate the request to a full blown audit. The usual sequence of a regulatory audit are as follows (DOL and IRS audits are fundamentally similar):

1. Notification of an investigation;

2. Document and interview discovery;

3. Analysis of evidence;

4. Notification of findings;

5. Resolution.

In most cases, the agency will send a letter to the company informing them that an investigation is underway. This letter will request documentation and interviews with plan officials corresponding to a specific date. The documents requested are usually lengthy, and may include documents going back anywhere from three to six years. The statute of limitations for retirement plans is six years, although how this applies is currently under review by the Supreme Court of the United States.

When the investigation letter is received, it is time to begin coordinating with service providers, advisors, consultants, and especially ERISA attorneys. Getting everyone involved early in the process is paramount to getting through an audit under the best possible circumstances. At this time, the plan officials should designate a "contact person" through which all correspondence and documentation should flow—generally speaking, an ERISA attorney.

The document collection and interview will typically be requested at the company's location, but you may be able to negotiate this based on the circumstances. The timeframe for producing the documents may be very short, usually between 10-15 days from the postmark, but again, this can be negotiated if more time is needed.

The agency, particularly the DOL, will almost never disclose the nature of the investigation, what precipitated it, or what violations they are looking for. Some insight may be gained by narrowing the scope of the document request. The request usually covers a broad scope of documents, but the plan officials can request clarification for specific documents. Correspondence regarding any extensions or clarification should be made in writing by certified mail and records of correspondence should be retained.

Prior to the actual meeting, a few things should be considered. Good faith efforts for requests from the agency should always be implemented. Key employees should be notified what is about to take place. Auditors should be treated amicably, less you gain their ire which will not help you in the process. Anyone designated to welcome, escort or otherwise assist the investigator should keep any conversation not essential to the investigation to a minimum.

Even though you should be cordial to the investigator, you and your key employees should keep in mind that this is a legally adversarial situation. Always try to control the environment by taking steps to ensure that investigators are not able to speak with personnel not integral to the investigation process.

Secure and organize the requested documents, and make sure not to provide any information extraneous to the scope of the investigation unless it is specifically requested. When the meeting takes place, you should have any service providers integral to the process available, if they can contribute, based on the advice of your ERISA attorney. Do not provide any extra information or responses beyond what is asked.

Understand that the analysis by the investigator may take some time, and do not be pushy about a resolution. Investigators often have many cases at once, and frequently more prominent cases may take precedent over yours. Give the investigator the time to complete his/her duties.

When the investigation is concluded, a letter will be sent to the company regarding the agency's findings. Often this will incorporate "voluntary corrections," particularly with DOL investigations. These are not idle recommendations. The DOL will expect you to implement the corrective procedures and provide evidence of the same. You can disagree with their findings with supporting evidence in writing and eventually come to a mutually agreeable conclusion. Most DOL cases that cannot arrive at an agreeable resolution will be resolved in civil court.

The 20% disgorgement penalty for the DOL will usually only apply if a formal settlement is made or by litigation. Make sure that any "voluntary corrective" measures are not part of a formal settlement to avoid the 20% penalty. Again, a good ERISA attorney and competent service providers will help you through this process.

The IRS closing process is a little different. Facts and circumstances must be agreed to by both parties in order to reach a settlement. If they cannot agree, the issues are renegotiated with IRS management or counsel, all the way up to the IRS chief counsel. If an agreement still cannot be reached, the plan is at risk for tax status disqualification, which is the worst possible outcome. If an agreement is reached, it will fall under the audit closing agreement program, which will usually result in fines, restitutions, and/or penalties that are less severe than disqualification, but worse than if the plan had taken voluntary corrective measures prior to the audit.

The IRS and the DOL can and will communicate with each other and if one agency finds potential issues in an area not under their jurisdiction, they will most certainly notify the corresponding agency.

Having basic documentation controls in place and using competent service providers, advisors and attorneys can minimize and control the damage from an investigation and result in an outcome beneficial to everyone involved.

Best Practices

Fiduciary Delegation Issues

The role of the plan administrator is the most likely fiduciary position to see problems or failures associated with fiduciary responsibilities that have been delegated to other personnel. Failures of delegation almost always occur in-house with employees who play some role in assisting with the administration of the plan.

Examine exactly what functions of the plan administrator have been delegated to in-house personnel (human resources), and to what extent control or discretion involving plan management and operation has been given in the course of that delegation. Ministerial functions that do not involve control or discretion (such as tracking data, documentation efforts, etc.) are less susceptible to fiduciary failures, but nevertheless should be monitored for accuracy and effect. Any fiduciary functions that are delegated need to be reviewed in accordance with prudent processes described in previous sections.

Plan administrators have many responsibilities, and it is often unreasonable to assume that any one person can handle it all. Plan officials should seriously consider the use of a fiduciary committee in managing the responsibilities of the administrator, where delegation can be more carefully controlled and coordinated.

Engage the TPA

The TPA is usually the best source of assistance for any kind of administrative issue. Be proactively engaged with the TPA throughout the relationship by:

- Knowing the deadlines for certain testing requirements;
- Discussing plan compliance issues regularly;
- Alert the TPA regarding any legal structure, ownership, or organizational change in the business;
- Ensuring testing results are reported, documented and filed in your due diligence file;
- Regularly conducting plan document reviews (as IRS rules often changes requiring plan document amendments by certain deadlines);
- And ask questions!

Reporting Company Census Information Accurately to Your TPA

Company census information needs to be accurately reported timely to the TPA or service provider responsible for ongoing determination to ensure that participant eligibility, participation and vesting schedules are determined properly. Plan sponsors also need to carefully review any reports or documents prepared by the TPA.

Any errors discovered in that information should be immediately reported to the TPA and plan administrator. Inaccurate eligibility, participation, and vesting calculations continue to be a major source of compliance failures according to the IRS, with most of the failures resulting from incorrect information being communicated between the plan sponsor and the service provider.

TRAP #28

FAILING TO REMIT CONTRIBUTIONS IN A TIMELY MANNER

Still cited as a leading source of plan compliance failures, plan sponsors must have a system in place to ensure coordination between payroll or payroll service providers and the plan/trust to ensure that contributions are remitted within the regulatory framework, and document when and why any failures or irregularities occur.

Pay Attention to Compensation and Payroll Issues

Whether a business has its own payroll department or outsources some or part of those services, it is extremely important to have a system of checks and balances in place to ensure that:

1. Participant eligibility is tracked and accurately reported to the service provider;

2. Definition of compensation per the payroll department/ service is consistent with the definition of compensation in the plan document;

3. Contributions are being correctly accounted for and deducted;

4. And contributions are being timely and correctly deposited.

As a best practice to avoid depositing employee deferrals late, keep a record of the withholding dates and corresponding deposit dates, note the shortest period, and try and keep contribution deposits at the shortest period, and document circumstances that arose when deposits took longer.[50] If you can demonstrate to an auditor that you were

---

50 Dacey, D.R. (2010). *Fiduciary Duty and Timeliness of Participant 401(k) Deposits.* WithumSmith+Brown, PC.

aware of the rules, took steps to ensure the funds were consistently reasonably segregated, and had extenuating circumstances at times when the deposits were later (but still within the maximum time based on plan size), you are much less likely to be accused of committing a prohibited transaction.

Finally if you know that you won't be able to deposit the funds within the required time, you can apply for an extension for up to ten days with the DOL. However, the requirements are complex and include a very specific disclosure requirement to participants within a specified time, receipt of an irrevocable letter of credit or performance bond prior to the extension, and within a specific timeframe provide evidence to the government that you completed the required steps. For more information about what is required to file an extension, see 29 CFR 2510.3-102(d).

Use Third Party Assistance with Completing the 5500

Third party assistance for completion of the 5500 is almost always utilized unless the plan sponsor has the expertise in house. I am often asked how the administrator can ensure the accuracy of the 5500 when they don't have the expertise to know any better. This is a great question, and difficult to answer, but at a minimum you should:

1. Ensure that the service provider responsible for 5500 preparation was properly vetted before contracting with them (a legal requirement anyway) by comparing other providers, determining experience and expertise, checking references, internet searches, analysis of the SAS 70 Type II, etc.;

2. Ensure all reporting documentation provided by you to the service provider is accurate;

3. Review you financial records to ascertain the validity and accuracy of any supporting documentation sent by any service provider that would be used for the 5500;

4. Review the 5500 for inaccuracies, discrepancies, etc.;

5. Ask questions and insist on answers;

6. Make sure you FILE the 5500 because that responsibility usually rests with the plan administrator;

7. DOCUMENT THE PROCESS...due diligence is meaningless if you can't prove you actually did it!

Having an Employee Sign the 5500 who is Not the Named Administrator in the Plan Documents

Too often, especially with small businesses, an employee who is typically an HR or office manager, who is not the named administrator in the plan documents, will sign the 5500. This is often done because the named administrator has delegated the responsibility for signing the 5500 to the employee because they are too busy to review and sign it themselves. This is especially prevalent in medical practices.

In the opinion of many legal experts, signing the 5500 as the administrator is an acknowledgment of fiduciary responsibility in accordance with the functions of the plan administrator. Thus in signing that document as the administrator, the employee may unwillingly and unknowingly subject themselves to all of the responsibility and liability of the same. At the same time, this does not disavow the named administrator from any responsibility or liability in that delegation.

Plan administrators should be wary about allowing a delegated employee to sign the 5500 on behalf of the named administrator, particularly when the delegated employee is inappropriately delegated and does not have the knowledge or skill to verify the information contained in the 5500. This is an all too common practice, and one that should be avoided unless that employee has the requisite skill to evaluate the 5500 and acknowledges their fiduciary duties in writing or by process and procedure.

Record Required Document Distributions

You may want to consider implementing a system that documents the sending and/or constructive receipt for required participant and beneficiary literature discussed herein. However, be cautious to ensure that you timely deliver the notices according to the rules.

Consider Issuing Blackout Notices "Just in Case"

The issue regarding blackout notices and the "3 day" rule can cause problems when the intended blackout period is within the three days, but for whatever reasons ends up taking longer. The DOL provides a very limited safe harbor for a failure under this circumstance. You can still be held accountable if the blackout period extends beyond three days and you did not distribute the required notices.

Obey the Disclosure Distribution Rules

The simplest of best practices: know the disclosure distribution rules and obey them! Use a checklist, calendar, or get help from a vendor such as a TPA or consultant.

Get Expert Assistance with the new ERISA 404(a) 5 Requirements

The new participant disclosure requirements will generally be provided by other service providers. Although the administrator can "reasonably rely" on its accuracy under the right circumstances, it is the administrator's responsibility to ensure all the requisite disclosures are made. You can find various checklists and other information on the internet, but close coordination with a competent advisor can help you ensure that the right disclosures are being made.

TRAP #29

NOT ACTING ON PARTICIPANT CONCERNS AND COMPLAINTS

By its own admission, the DOL reports that one of the greatest reasons for plan audit engagements comes from participant complaints to the agency. These complaints may be the result of participant frustration from the handling of the concerns at the company level. Have a documented process in place to address participant concerns and complaints in a thorough and efficient manner, thereby lessening the chance that the participant escalates the complaint to the DOL.

Act on Participant Inquires and Complaints

One of the largest precipitators for a DOL investigation will come from a participant making a complaint to the DOL. The DOL does not automatically initiate an investigation over any one compliant but if there are multiple complaints, a pattern exists or claims of gross impropriety are made, then that may justify a full scale investigation. Often the DOL will simply attempt to clear up a participants misunderstandings about their rights and/or benefits, or request feedback from the employer if the issue is not clearly resolved.

It's widely believed that some plans will experience some "push back" from participants when they see the participant fee disclosures on their individual statements for the first time. It's important to have a system in place to document any inquires or complaints made to an officer of the plan, and a follow up system for resolving the issue to the best of your ability. Equally important is the need to timely disclose other records requests by participants for which they have the right to inspect.

Be Careful Administering Loans and Hardship Distributions

The regulating agencies are paying particular attention to the administration of loans and hardship distributions because of a track record of problems related to the same. Some TPAs will assist with loan administration, but at the end of the day you must comply with ERISA and IRC rules related to loan amounts, frequencies, accessibility, etc. Hardship provisions, if allowed, must follow strict IRC guidelines that the plan administrator is responsible for adhering to. Loans and hardship distributions will be discussed in greater detail in the next section.

Document Retention Requirements

There are two requirements per ERISA relating to document retention: Section 107 and Section 209. Section 107 requires that all records pertaining to regulatory agency filings or to participant or beneficiary disclosures must be retained and kept available for examination for a minimum of six years after the filing date. However Section 209 of ERISA requires that employers keep benefit records for all employees required for determination of benefits due or may become due, and further DOL clarification seems to indicate that this period of time is indefinite, or at least until the records become irrelevant for benefit determination.

In one notable situation the courts ruled against the employer for failing to maintain records consistent with Section 209's requirement. In general, be cautious about destroying records related to benefits owed to participants or beneficiaries. In theory, any records related to regulating agency disclosure requirements, such as the form 5500, its various incarnations and supporting documents, would probably fall under the 107 requirements, while any other records should be carefully scrutinized to determine if they have any relevancy to benefit determination before being destroyed.

TRAP #30

FAILING TO PROPERLY TERMINATE A PLAN OR FAILING TO RECOGNIZE WHEN A PARTIAL PLAN TERMINATION HAS OCCURRED

Failures in plan terminations are common problem, and plan fiduciaries should understand that just because a decision has been made to terminate the plan does not mean that the responsible fiduciaries do not have an obligation to ensure that the termination is carried out properly. Partial plan terminations are not widely understood, but nevertheless the plan fiduciaries are responsible for recognizing when partial terminations take place and taking action to ensure beneficiaries receive benefits that they may be due.

Full and Partial Plan Terminations

A retirement plan is terminated when the sponsoring employer makes a settlor decision to cease operating the plan. Although the actual decision to terminate a plan is not fiduciary in nature, the actual process involved in executing the termination will most certainly involve fiduciary decisions and processes.

The process should be carefully coordinated between all of the existing service providers to ensure everyone is on the same page and working towards the same goal of getting all of the assets in the plan to the appropriate beneficiaries. Plan sponsors should only file a terminated "final filing" form 5500 when there are no assets remaining in the plan.

Plan sponsors need to be aware of partial terminations and what it means for them. A partial termination can occur when a plan sees a reduction in the number of participants by way of plan amendment or corporate action, such as layoffs or restructuring. The generally accepted threshold by the courts and IRS is a reduction in participation by 20% or more.

A big remaining question concerns the reduction time frame. Recent district court decisions have indicated that corporate actions can take place over many years, so the reduction resulting in a partial termination theoretically could take place over just one year or many years. This is a facts and circumstances decision, and usually it is the corporation that needs to make the first decision about whether a plan participation reduction qualifies as a partial termination.

The consequences of a partial termination are that certain participants in the plan "affected" by the termination will require an acceleration of vested benefits regardless of the vesting schedule; this means affected participants are 100% vested on the date of the partial termination so that employer contributions are not forfeited. Employers have the obligation to determine which employees are considered "affected", and to restore forfeited balances for determined "affected" participants. Vesting failures can be corrected through the IRS by using the Voluntary Correction Program.

Consult a Legal and/or Tax Professional for Corrections

And finally, as if not emphasized enough, consult with a legal and/or tax professional proficient in ERISA matters for any errors or prohibited transactions and any efforts involving resolution with the EPCRS, the DFVCP or the VFCP!

Summary

The rules and regulations discussed in this section are administrative duties, and therefore the responsibility of the plan administrator. This role cannot be overstated. Although you will find that service providers such as TPAs, record keepers, and trustees can assist with the disclosure requirements, the ultimate responsibility for the accuracy and timeliness of the disclosures always rests on the shoulders of the administrator. Therefore it is critical that the plan administrator understand his responsibility and keep an accurate accounting and log of disclosures made and stay consistent with ERISA.

Employee complaints to the DOL are the one of the largest sources of enforcement actions, so it is critical to supply participants and beneficiaries with the appropriate disclosures in a timely fashion and deal proactively with internal participant complaints. This includes handling IRS and DOL disclosures, namely the Form 5500. Following best practices, policies and procedures can go a long way to ensuring that the plan is being run smoothly.

In the event that problems do arise, it's all the more critical to follow the DOL and IRS guidelines for correcting plan problems. Ignoring administrative failures may seem like the easiest thing to do, but the consequences can be very severe absent corrective procedures. Fortunately the regulating bodies offer standard, relatively easy to follow rules for correcting plan problems. As with anything else, consult an attorney or consultant with expertise with ERISA issues before attempting to correct any problems yourself.

CORE ELEMENT 6: PLAN HEALTH AND PERFORMANCE

Consider the following scenario: You are at Los Angeles International Airport in the terminal waiting to board a flight to Orlando with your family. While you are waiting, the gate attendant makes the following announcement to everyone waiting in the passenger concourse:

"Dear ladies and gentlemen, welcome to Acme Airlines. We are honored you have chosen us for your air carrier. We would like to relay a brief message from the pilot. He wanted you all to know that although Acme Airlines strives to get all of our passengers to their destinations, there is a 40% chance we will not arrive at our destination on time or safely. We hope you enjoy your flight and will begin boarding shortly!"

Are you getting on that plane with your family?

This is exactly the scenario the American worker is facing with their retirement. Is your business an Acme Airline, or do you have what it takes to help get those who are willing to commit to saving for retirement a chance to get to their destination on time and safely?

* *

The final core element is unfortunately one of the most ignored elements, yet may be the most likely to help the plan achieve its objectives. Plan health concerns the overall productivity of the plan and its participants, while performance refers to meeting goals and objectives, not necessarily investment returns. The goals of this section are to:

✓ Review the importance of plan health and performance;

✓ Learn the importance of setting annual plan goals;

✓ Discuss how to measure plan performance;

✓ Learn about optional features to improve plan performance;

✓ Discuss the participants education needs;

✓ Review other features that can affect the plan's performance and participant access.

TRAP #31

FAILING TO MONITOR PLAN HEALTH AND PERFORMANCE

Many companies don't have a process for monitoring the health and performance of the plan with respect to its goals and objectives, whether those goals are getting the most benefit to the top earners, getting everyone to retirement, or providing an incentive that outpaces your competition.

Why Health and Performance Matters

Plan health and performance is an important element to a successful plan because ultimately, the objective is to provide a benefit to employees and if they are unable or unwilling to take advantage of those benefits, then it begs the question of why the benefit exists in the first place. Gauging plan health and driving performance help to ensure that the plan is improving and maturing. Failing to do so can lead to stagnation and eventually create more of a problem for the business than a benefit to the employee.

For most plans, the ultimate objective is to get the employee to a point where they can replace a sufficient amount of income to retire. Getting employees to retirement is not only a moral victory, but a tangible one for the business. Numerous studies point to the rising costs of an aging workforce. As a workforce ages, productivity declines and the risk of workman's compensation and disability claims increases. Older workers typically command more pay and cost more in terms of insurance benefits. Therefore businesses that can help employees get to retirement on time will have a younger, more productive, and less expensive workforce.

Also, a well-managed plan can be a great tool for recruiting and retaining talent. Staying on top of how your plan fits compared with your industry peer groups and your competitors can give you a competitive advantage in acquiring talent. And finally, a plan with high participation and contribution rates will be less likely to fail any of the key compliance tests, thereby allowing the owners and key employers to maximize their own retirement savings.

The first step is to do an initial analysis of the plan, comparing it with peer groups and similar size/types of plans. This is a snapshot, broad overview of the general plan health. Things such as plan design features, contribution and participation rates, investment options, fees, and other metrics are typically used to make this initial analysis. Once this analysis is made, you can determine inefficiencies, failures, and setbacks, as well as plan features that are working well, and begin to formulate a plan for improvement.

Measuring Health and Performance

Although there is no specific requirement to measure a plan's "overall" performance, it's important for the plan officials to have some grasp on how the plan is moving in relation to the original goals for starting the plan in the first place. In my opinion, the ultimate goal is to get every single one of your employees to a comfortable retirement, but that is a tremendously unlikely scenario for most businesses for a multitude of reasons. So maybe the focus should be on giving them the tools, resources, and direction to help make them successful in *saving* for retirement.

Some thoughts about deciding on what easily determinable metrics are important:

- As a fiduciary, it *must* be your goal to defray expenses, but to what limit? Is choosing the cheapest service provider necessarily prudent in and of itself? Probably not. We should be seeking value and benefits in the services we need for the plan, not necessarily the least expensive.

- Part of defraying expenses comes into play by the size of the plan itself; larger plans can generally demand better price points. So should a goal be to grow the assets of the plan? If so what is the best way to accomplish that?

- How much should the employer contribute to plan expenses? Is it reasonable to expect the participants to pay for the entire benefit? If the employer will contribute, what is the best use of those dollars?

- Does your participation rate mirror similar size plans in similar industry groups? Low participation will impact plan performance, decrease contribution limits for the highly compensated, and decrease the sense of value for the plan among the workforce. How can you drive participation and get more people involved in taking control of their future?

- Are you able to contribute as much as you want, or are you limited because of plan design, participation, or some other reason? How do we get you to be able to contribute more for yourself and your partners without being so generous to everyone else that you feel like you're giving everything away?

And some thoughts about certain metrics that are less easily determined:

- How do the participants view this plan? How do I demonstrate the value of this benefit to the whole workforce? You created a benefit, paid start-up expenses and on-going expenses, and absorbed a lot of liability to provide this benefit, and you should want your workforce to recognize that commitment to them and sacrifice on your part.

- Will just contributing be enough to drive the participant's retirement outcome? Is there something else I can provide without incurring more costs?

While the subject of defraying expenses is covered in depth in Core Element Three "Service Provider Retention", the rest of these thoughts are real considerations affecting plan sponsors every day. A good plan consultant or advisor can help you determine what metrics are most important for your plan and give you tools necessary to help your plan deliver the benefit it was designed to provide.

Setting Annual Plan Goals

Once the initial analysis is complete, the plan's fiduciaries and stewards should begin considering what improvements should be made, how that will be accomplished, and how successes or failures will be measured. These goals should be made annually if practical, worked on throughout the plan year, and reviewed and modified subsequently to continually improve the plan. Demonstrating concern over the health of the plan and documenting actions taken to improve the plan go a long way in demonstrating prudent processes.

Driving Plan Performance

Plan performance can be measured by evaluating how successful the plan is at achieving its goals. Since the primary function of a retirement plan is to get your employees to retirement, the success or failure of that effort should be a primary metric for evaluation. The success or failure can be determined by evaluating participant outcomes, particularly as to whether or not an employee has reached an asset base sufficient to generate an income replacement to allow them to retire with roughly the standard of living they desire.

So a primary goal in driving plan performance is to get the employee to save enough to retire, but herein lies the problem: employers cannot control the savings habits of their employees. Although this is true, there are some considerations that should be made to implementing programs designed to take the decision, at least initially, out of the hands of the employee.

Getting Employees to Retirement by Improving Participant Outcomes

Ultimately, participant outcomes are the name of the game. And there are a variety of tools we have available to help get our employees to retirement. Some are an "easy" button, and others will require more work, but all should be evaluated to determine if they have a role to play in the plan.

An important, but often ignored and difficult to assess metric, is determining the progress towards getting a replacement income sufficient to retire. We typically look at income replacement ratio projections. These projections vary in form, but generally take individual savings and matching rates, apply some assumptions with regards to inflation and investment performance and compare the projected income replacement with their current income thereby giving a percent of current income likely to be replaced. This gives us a general measure of what percentage of income they are likely to replace if they continue their current habits.

Income replacement ratios give a tangible meaning for participants in terms of what savings and contributions will likely result for them in real monthly dollars ten, twenty, or thirty years down the road. It's an important concept for them to understand to begin a discussion about improving savings or investing habits. Service providers often provide tools and calculators to help the employee conceptualize the required assets and corresponding savings rates to get to a desired outcome. The DOL has realized the importance of getting employees to understand these requirements, and regulations are likely forthcoming that may require more access to these tools.

Unsurprisingly, even with these calculators many employees will feel overwhelmed at the proposition of a gigantic hurdle that they must overcome, particularly if they are starting late. This feeling can overwhelm them into doing nothing at all out of fear and frustration. Having a participant level advisor available to help them ascertain the totality of their situation, encourage savings and bring some measure of reality can go a long way in helping employees to help themselves even in light of painful realties. Nevertheless, plan sponsors have some tools available to them to overcome an employee's indecision.

Increasing Your Ability to Contribute: Auto Enrollment and Auto Escalation

Auto enrollment and auto escalation features provide alternatives for plans that suffer from low enrollment or contributions.

Eligible Automatic Contribution Arrangements (EACA), also known as auto enrollment, causes any eligible employee to be enrolled into the plan automatically unless the employee specifically opts out.

Qualified Automatic Contribution Arrangements (QACA), also known as auto escalation (or auto increase) features permit the plan periodically to increase the participants contribution to the plan up to a certain level, unless the participant opts not to participate or designates a different (or same) contribution level.

Safe harbors exist for the construction of the auto enrollment and auto escalation features that require notices to be provided to the participants, but they are beyond the scope of this text so as usual consult with a plan advisor or service provider with regards to the construction and disclosure requirements. Failure to remain within the safe harbor limitations can result in unintended liability exposure for plan fiduciaries.

The value of these features may not be intuitively obvious to the uninitiated, but the consequence for the employee pool is getting more people enrolled and getting more people's contributions to levels that may produce a better retirement outcome. There also may be significant benefits for the highly compensated or key personnel whose contributions are tested against the non-highly compensated. This often results in those employee/owners being able to contribute more to their own accounts without failing the anti-discrimination testing associated with their contribution levels.

TRAP #32

FAILING TO ACCOUNT FOR THE PARTICIPANT EXPERIENCE AND PROVIDING BASIC INVESTMENT EDUCATION

Ultimately, it's about the participants and getting them closer to retirement. Since participant complaints are a significant source for regulatory engagement, it makes sense to be sure that the participants and beneficiaries understand and respect the value of the benefit you are providing for them.

Demonstrating Value: The Participant Experience

The goal for most plan sponsors is usually two-fold: provide a meaningful benefit for employees that contribute to the acquisition and retention of talent by getting employees on a path to retirement, and secondly to maximize benefits for the owners and key management. Seldom have I found many plan sponsors that actually take the time to measure what the experience is like for the participant; usually they only take notice when someone has something negative to say. Since participant and beneficiary complaints remain a significant source of DOL investigations, it behooves the plan sponsor to take notice to what the participants actually like about the plan, what they dislike, and what their attitudes towards saving and investing are to begin with.

One way to gauge the participant experience is to conduct periodic surveys with the participants about various aspects of the plan, their investment experience, etc. These surveys can easily be set up on a voluntary basis, and can provide great insight into how the workforce feels about their plan. You are not obligated to act on anything, but certain metrics can be important to knowing what the experience is like for them.

For instance, the most the participants are generally exposed to with regard to the plan's dynamics comes from the record keepers' client facing software and enrollment kits. Most participants today go online for information regarding their plan. If the record keeper's website is not easy to use or doesn't provide the right tools and otherwise negatively impacts the participants' experiences, it may be grounds to consider seeking another record keeper whose interface is more user friendly and provides an overall better experience for the participants.

Obviously, measuring participant experience is an important but possibly time consuming endeavor. Having the right plan level advisor to provide investment education and assist with the construction, delivery, interpretation, and follow-up of participant surveys can be useful for plan sponsors in qualifying what is important to participants and what is not.

Do not forget to include beneficiaries on accounts that remain under the plan when the participant has passed, become disabled, etc. These beneficiaries have generally the same rights as the participants, and can cause equal consternation for the plan if they are ignored.

Reducing the Risk of Poor Participant Investment Decisions with Education

The best way to ascertain the participant's experience is to be proactive and engaging. There are several ways to accomplish this. Providing investment education to participants on the basics of investing is a good start, especially at plan inception and throughout. Although not expressly required, many consider providing good education an ethical requirement if not a legal one.

Participant education can not only help an investor learn basic investing concepts, but it can also teach them about the typical behaviors and thought processes that cause investors to make poor long term investment decisions. Effective education should also reinforce the concept that deferral rates will contribute more to retirement outcomes than investment returns.

The good news is that record keepers and advisors are keenly aware of the need to deliver good educational materials, and a ton of good products are out there to achieve that goal. Advisors may play a role in providing on-site education and even one-on-one guidance, or they can often conduct meeting via online live video. Some record keepers provide more extensive educational resources than others, including on demand video libraries and staff to assist with enrollment and education.

TRAP #33

PROVIDING PARTICIPANT EDUCATION VS. ADVICE

Plan sponsors need to be cautious when administering participant education programs, particularly when participants seek education or advice in-house. Giving general information about investing concepts is educational and thus non-fiduciary in nature, but anyone giving specific advice can find themselves a functional investment advisory fiduciary. Leave the investment advice to the professionals.

A word of caution: the DOL provides insight into what constitutes investment "education" versus investment "advice". Giving investment "advice" can impart unintended liabilities to the plan sponsor, specifically drawing them into the domain of the 3(21)(A)(ii) investment advisor fiduciary, something plan sponsors should avoid specifically because most are not qualified to give that kind of specific advice. The DOL's interpretive bulletin IB 96-1 spells out specific subjects that constitute "education" versus advice which will keep the plan sponsor out of the area of fiduciary liability with respect to that.[51]

Education Policy Statements

The concept of plan sponsors creating a policy statement for participant education is a relatively new development in the retirement plan space. Although not specifically required under ERISA, it is being seen as a best practice for plans to consider adopting and some experts believe employee education is a basic fiduciary responsibility. The reason behind this concept is due to the general lack of investor education and sophistication, particularly for plan participants who have all of their retirement assets invested in an employer sponsored plan and otherwise have little access to professional financial advice.

If you are going to implement an education policy statement, you should first consider the overall plan demographics and sophistication of the employee group and what you want to achieve. The next step is to determine how you are going to go about reaching those objectives, and how you will benchmark successes and failures. Finally, you should be open to adjusting the level of education as the sophistication and experience of the participants increase. Be careful that you create a course of action that is reasonable to achieve; you don't want to create a policy that you later violate.

For more information about what constitutes participant education, consult the DOL's Interpretive Bulletin 96-1.

51   United States Department of Labor. (1996). *EBSA Final Rules*. Retrieved from United States Department of Labor: www.dol.gov/ebsa/regs/fedreg/final/96_14093.pdf

TRAP #34

IMPROPER USE OR CONTROL OVER ACCESSIBILITY OPTIONS THAT CAUSE LEAKAGE FROM THE PLAN

Some optional plan features can improve participant access to their assets in the plan, but other features can counteract against the goals of the plan while creating an administrative headache. Plan sponsor need to carefully weigh whether or not to incorporate these features.

Managing Plan Leakage

Plan leakage refers to reductions in plan assets as a result of participant accessibility to those assets, particularly in the form of cash-outs, loans, in-service withdrawals, and rollovers. The plan sponsor has discretion over many of these features, and in order for them to be implemented they must be permitted by the plan documents in the initial draft or by amendment. As such these features could have been included in the "Administration" section, but due to their impact on plan health and performance the decision was made to address them in this section.

The subject of whether to provide cash-outs, loans and in-service withdrawals are controversial at best. While the law requires certain distributions to be made available (e.g. distributions as a result of disability or death) the others are mostly optional plan design features. Loans and hardship distributions can be especially difficult to manage administratively, and both are subject to special rules in regards to their form and function.

Cash-Outs

Cash-outs come in two flavors: voluntary and involuntary. Voluntary cash-outs are made by the participant when the participant is no longer eligible to contribute to the plan, usually due to severance. A participant then makes the decision to "cash-out" the balance, with all taxes and penalties due, or "rollover" the balance to an eligible IRA or 401(k) plan with a new employer.

Voluntary cash-outs are the most common and unpreventable forms of plan leakage. Voluntary cash-outs are sometimes beneficial to the plan, especially due to the fact that the administrator is still responsible for disclosure requirements for beneficiaries, who may become difficult to locate or communicate with. Even though an employee may have terminated service with the employer (thus becoming a plan beneficiary instead of participant), the plan still has a fiduciary responsibility to that beneficiary as long as they maintain an account balance with the plan. Allowing those assets to leave the plan absolve the fiduciary of any ongoing responsibility, and thus it may be best that most of those assets eventually leave.

Involuntary cash-outs are an optional design feature that allow a plan to expel certain account balances under minimum amounts. Any account balance in excess of $5,000 will require a voluntary election of any cash-out, but balances under $5,000 can be cashed out by the employer when a participant terminates employment. Any balances between $1,000 and $5,000 are required to be "rolled" into an eligible IRA for the benefit of the employee in order to avoid taxes and/or penalties, unless elected otherwise by the employee.

Account balances under $1,000 can be cashed out regardless of tax consequences to the employee. The practice of using involuntary cash-outs is commonplace due to the administrative costs associated with managing multiple micro accounts with no future contributions. Particular fee arrangements, such as per capita flat fees, can quickly decimate a small account balance, so it is a best practice to evaluate the benefits and drawbacks for involuntary cash-out options.

Loans

Loans are generally not desirable for a plan because they interfere in the primary purpose of the plan: to provide retirement benefits to the participants upon separation of service. Many participants take advantage of loans because they incorrectly view it as asset providing benefits that it isn't designed to provide. The ultimate decision rests with the plan sponsor with regards to whether to permit loans across the plan or not, and that may be dependent on the demographics and needs of the employees.

Allowing participants access to loans can be viewed as an added benefit, but this often results in reduced account individual balances and an administrative headache for the sponsor. Additionally, employees who fail to pay back the loan in time may be subject to taxes and penalties.

Plan sponsors can restrict loan access for certain circumstances. Loans must be paid back to the plan within five years, with some exceptions. If a participant has no outstanding loans, the IRC sets a maximum amount of a loan up to 50% of the vested balance but no more than $50,000. Loans are charged an interest rate, usually the prime rate plus one percent.

Multiple loans within a twelve month period are typically not allowed. By regulation, loans are not allowed from IRAs, SEPs and SIMPLE IRAs, and loans from a 401(k) cannot be rolled into the same. If a loan is not repaid within the allotted time frame or a participant terminates employment, any unpaid loan amount is distributed to the employee as income, subject to taxes and penalties if applicable. Refer to www. irs.gov/Retirement-Plans/Retirement-Plans-FAQs-regarding-Loans for more information on loans from retirement plans.

Recently loans have been the focus of increased scrutiny and oversight due to persistent administrative errors in managing the loan process. Plans with a large amount of outstanding loans compared with assets in the plan may become a target for an auditor. In general, when loans exceed 10% of overall plan assets, the plan sponsor may need to re-evaluate the loan policies.

In-Service Withdrawals

In-service withdrawals are another consideration for the plan sponsor. In-service withdrawals generally allow a participant to withdrawal, transfer or rollover a portion of their assets upon hardship or attainment of a certain age.

Plan sponsors should be cautious about allowing in-service withdrawals not only to prevent plan leakage, but because of increased administrative burdens they will be responsible for, especially concerning hardship withdrawals. Also a plan with an aging workforce with one or both of these alternatives available may lose significant assets at a critical time, which could impose higher fees on all the participants due to economics of scale and loss of bargaining power with the service providers.

Age Attained Distributions

In-service age attainment withdrawals are withdrawals or rollovers permitted upon attainment of a certain age, usually from age 59 ½ to age 65. Permitting in-service age attainment withdrawals may allow a participant to move a portion of their assets into another income producing product prior to retirement, which may be especially important for participants looking for guaranteed income alternatives, such as an annuity, that may not otherwise be available under the plan.

Plan sponsors can permit this options for any one or all eligible retirement accounts that a participant has with the company, but in-service withdrawals generally restricted to vested, non-elective contributions.

Hardship Distributions

Contrary to popular belief, hardship distributions are not required to be provided in company sponsored retirement plans. The discretion as to whether or not to offer them rests solely with the employer. If an employer chooses to allow this option they must understand the rules regarding hardships, abide by those rules and the permissions in the plan document, and make an effort to internally document the process and justification for the hardship distribution.

The IRS has special rules about hardship distributions. They are:

1. The withdrawal is due to a "heavy" and "immediate" need (certain safe harbor reasons to follow);

2. There are no other resources available to satisfy the need (other plan distributions, including loans, must have been utilized with certain limited exceptions);

3. The amount withdrawn must not exceed the amount required to meet the need.

In order to satisfy the heavy and immediate need required, the IRS recognizes typically six safe harbor reasons to allow hardship withdrawals:

- Unreimbursed medical expenses per IRC 213(d) for the participant, spouse or dependents;

- Purchasing an employee's principal residence;

- Educational expenses for the next 12 months for the participant, spouse, or dependents;

- Payments to prevent eviction or foreclosure on the principal residence;

- Funeral expenses for the participant, spouse or dependent;

- Certain expenses to repair a participant's principal residence.

Like age attained in-service distributions, plan sponsors have leeway in deciding what assets are eligible for hardship withdrawal per the plan document. Administrators need to take steps to ensure that extra due diligence is achieved because of the burden the IRS places on the plan administrator to determine and document the need. The hardship policy should be clear with easy to implement processes and procedures. Please refer to www.irs.gov/Retirement-Plans/Retirement-Plans-FAQs-regarding-Hardship-Distributions for additional guidance.

Participants should be required to provide substantial and concrete evidence of the hardship need and lack of resources. If the administrator fails to ascertain the legitimacy of the claim, the plan can be subject to enforcement action. The IRS is cognizant of failures in the industry in administering hardship distributions, and plan administrators need to be aware that this can be a focal point of any investigation. Please refer to www.irs.gov/Retirement-Plans/Hardship-Distribution-Tips-from-EP-Exam for additional guidance.

Rollovers

Rollovers are distributions into similar tax-qualified accounts, such as from a 401(k) to an IRA. Upon termination or in accordance with certain in-service withdrawal options, participants can "rollover" their assets into a "rollover IRA" without a tax consequence if done correctly. Rollovers are always permitted as long as the employee has a qualifying circumstance, such as separation from service.

Plan sponsors can choose whether or not to allow rollovers from other "like" qualified plans into the company plan for participants who have assets in another plan from a prior employer. Traditional contributory IRAs, setup by the account owner outside of company sponsored retirement plan that correspondingly receive contributions from the owner, are not allowed to be rolled into a company sponsored retirement plan but "rollover IRAs" may be allowed at the plan sponsor's discretion, in accordance with the plan documents. At the time of this writing, I have not heard any compelling arguments for not allowing rollovers into a plan, but the decision must be made by the plan sponsor with regards to the needs of the plan and its participants.

Summary

In this section we reviewed at a high level various types of plan design options that are commonly found. Which options are best suited for your company is a function of many different considerations, and best discovered with the help of professionals. An ERISA consultant can help you identify various third party administrators who can in turn help advise you as to the best options given your particular needs and circumstances.

Whatever options you decide to implement, it is important to make sure that plan provides the benefit it is intended to provide, that you have a measure with which to determine its successes and failures, and that you are able to demonstrate its value to your employees. If the goal of the plan is to get participants as close to "retirement ready" as possible, then maximizing plan performance should be an important goal and to that end the regulatory agencies and the industry has provided various tools at your disposal to encourage participants to take advantage of the benefit you are offering them. As with any benefit when the participant understands and respects its value, they are more likely to utilize it and appreciate your efforts to provide it.

WRAPPING IT UP

Bringing it all together, we can take away a few key ideas which motivated me to write this to begin with:

- Company sponsored retirement plans are a key component to getting the American workforce to retirement;

- Plan design is the first step to a successful retirement plan, and understanding what features will and won't work for your business is critical to getting the plan off to the right start;

- ERISA fiduciary duties should be well understood and practiced with a documented process that strives to adhere to those duties;

- Understanding the roles and responsibilities of all the players in a retirement plan is key to identifying risks to the plan and its fiduciaries;

- New legislation requires plan fiduciaries determine the necessity of service, reasonableness of contract, and especially the reasonableness of fee structures before and during contracting with any service providers paid for using plan assets;

- Investment management should be outsourced to competent and experienced managers whenever possible, and at a minimum plan fiduciaries should consult with an investment advisor if they retain that responsibility in-house;

- Plan administrators need to coordinate with other service providers to ensure that everyone understands what each other's roles and responsibilities are;

- Measuring and improving plan performance is critical to the ultimate goal of getting people to retirement, and performance should be measured and strive to be continuously improved.

There are numerous hurdles that make sponsoring a retirement plan a daunting prospect once you understand what you are up against, but the reality is that the industry is improving and some advisors are choosing to focus their business only in the retirement plan landscape, and thus are able to offer much more dedicated and knowledgeable service than ever before.

The rules and regulations are changing almost every year, and it's important to keep up to date and informed of changes to the industry and how it might affect your business. In doing so, we will be updating our website periodically with podcasts and short videos highlighting important legislative and legal updates as they become available.

If you got nothing else from this book, then just takeaway the good, the bad, and the ugly:

- THE GOOD: There is plenty of expert help out there if you know what to look for, and you don't necessarily have to open up your checkbook to get access to it.

- THE BAD: You must have a process for decision making and that process should be documented, and failing to follow a prudent process and document that process will open the door to enforcement action and/or litigation.

- THE UGLY: If you are a fiduciary to the plan, you have real and personal liability for fiduciary failures, and ignorance is not an excuse in the eyes of the DOL, IRS, and the courts.

Getting the Benefits of Good Plan Operation and Governance

On the cover of this book I offered you the opportunity to learn the secrets of how to lower risk, costs, and taxes while saving you time and money. So if it wasn't obvious how to achieve those goals by adhering to the six core elements of successful retirement plans, allow me to point out a couple of actionable items that may help you.

Lowering Risk

The best way to lower your risk in a retirement plan is to implement good fiduciary controls, outsource some of the investment liability to a third party while taking advantage of limited liability provisions of 404(c) and QDIAs in the investment lineup, have proper bonding and insurance in place, keep an administrative calendar to help you manage the disclosure deadlines, be responsive to participant/beneficiary inquiries and complaints, and retain the services of a good plan level advisor who can guide you through these steps.

And ultimately, if you feel the fiduciary administrative responsibilities are too much for you to handle, consider hiring a service provider who you can outsource most or all of the administrative responsibilities to, or consider participation in a Multiple Employer Plan where those administrative responsibilities are mostly outsourced.

Lowering Your Costs

Expenses are a fact of life with retirement plans, but what you pay for and how you pay for it really matters. So when it comes to lowering costs, first you need to understand fee structures and how you are going to pay. Once you understand the fee structures, you can determine the best structure for you and negotiate the best contract based on how you are going to pay.

Likewise, as the plan grows you should consider the reasonableness of asset based charges and negotiate with you current providers to constrain the costs. Much of the costs associated with recordkeeping concern the number of participants and the services offered to them, so higher individual account balances (which correspond to smaller numbers of participants) will typically generate more favorable pricing arrangements. Total assets in a plan matter when you are contracting with fiduciary service providers because of the inherent liability related to increasing assets under management, advisement or trust.

You also need to find the best value for the dollars you are spending. Going with the cheapest provider in the market is likely to create more problems than it's going to solve. At the same time, if you are willing to pay a little more, make sure you understand what you are getting for those extra dollars and whether those services are reasonable, necessary and add value to the plan.

Lowering Taxes

One fact about taxes: no one likes paying them! Clearly retirement plan benefits offer significant tax benefits to employers for contributions, but there are other ways to squeeze tax savings as we have discussed.

If you are eligible, make sure you take advantage of any tax credits available. Currently a non-refundable tax credit exists for costs related to plan start up and it can be credited over a three year period. It's not a major benefit, but make sure you take advantage of it to offset some of the startup costs.

Next, consider the benefit of paying some plan costs using the general assets of the company versus the assets of the plan. This has a twofold effect of removing some fiduciary liability (fiduciary liability is theoretically reduced for fees if they are paid by the sponsor and not the plan or participants) and possibly generating a tax deduction for the business, which in many cases makes more sense than paying expenses that are not deductible from plan assets where more often than not the business owners and management ends up paying a greater share of the costs because they have more assets in the plan.

Also consider whether a cash balance or defined benefit program may make sense as an additional benefit. Just the savings in payroll taxes alone are often enough to justify the ongoing costs. Many plan sponsors are amazed at how much tax savings can be realized through these plans, and with the right employee demographics these plans make perfect sense for many plan sponsors.

Finally, you can consider other options that were beyond the scope of this book, such as 401(h) medical reimbursement accounts, 831(b) captive insurance companies, and other more advanced planning benefits that generate tremendous tax deductions for the business and often work in tandem with retirement plans already provided.

Keeping More Money in Your Pocket

In making a business decision to implement a plan, a clear idea of what the costs may be is clearly a major consideration. This includes not just the costs associated with the plan itself, but also the costs related to contributions, eligibility tracking, legal expenses, etc. Without increasing your outlay, it is often possible to find some contributions that can be reallocated to the ownership, and that starts with plan design.

You need to have the proper plan designed from the outset, or re-evaluate the plan design to see how much of your total outlay can be shifted to the ownership and/or key management while staying in compliance with the IRS. Often times we can get more of that expense going for the benefit of the ownership just by tweaking the plan design.

Another way to get more money in your pocket is to drive the plan's performance, and I'm not speaking specifically about investment performance. Driving plan performance, in particular participation and contribution levels can significantly increase the amount of money that owners can contribute for themselves due to adjustments in the compliance testing requirement per the IRC. This creates a double benefit by increasing your contribution levels while getting your employees onboard with the value of the benefit you are providing.

Gaining More Time for Yourself

The time required to spend on retirement plan management is a major obstacle for many employers, and can often lead an employer to reject setting up a plan in the first place. The good news is that you can squeeze more time out for yourself by sharing the load with competent service providers and none more so than a good plan advisor.

Some advisors will offer both fiduciary and non-fiduciary services to the plan, and some services can have a big impact on the amount of time you spend on the plan. Plan sponsors often spend more time than they should focusing on issues they don't fully understand as opposed to contracting with an advisor or consultant who can guide them through the complex tasks and help outsource or delegate the less important functions and oversight.

TRAP #35

HIRING THE WRONG ADVISOR

The wrong advisor is an advisor who's function doesn't formally and demonstrably improve the plan, its operations, and its value. Many advisors only dabble in the retirement plan business, and while they may know about investments they often don't know enough about retirement plans to be of any real benefit or in a worst case be a detriment to the plan. Hiring an advisor who only dabbles in retirement plan business is akin to hiring a plumber to build a house; he may know his trade and know it well, but he's not going to learn enough overnight to build you the house you want, and he probably knows just enough to be dangerous.

The Valued Advisor

A common theme throughout this book is the need for plan sponsors to get help with issues they don't understand. Part of your core fiduciary duties demands that you seek expert advice on matters outside your areas of expertise. For this reason a good advisor, plan consultant, and attorney can mean the difference between a successful, well managed plan and a plan heading for disaster. Unfortunately, many advisors only dabble in the retirement plan business and while their intentions are good, many are not the best choice to be advising plan sponsors.

Most advisors are paid for their services either by direct billing (usually a fiduciary) or revenue sharing arrangements. Since plan fiduciaries have a responsibility to evaluate all fees paid to all service providers, it is important for plan sponsors to evaluate the quality of service being provided by an advisor to what they are being compensated with by the plan. And if the advisor isn't living up to expectations, it's probably time to have a conversation with him or her and look at other options.

CORE6

That is why we developed our CORE6 service model, based on the six core elements of successful retirement plan management. We can help you and even help your advisors to better serve you. We understand that sometimes the relationship with an advisor or broker is long established, and that sometimes those relationships are valuable in other ways. We are open to helping other advisors improve their service to you. The offer exists nonetheless, and you can reach out to us through the following:

Email: adickens@mysummitwealth.com

Phone: (407) 656-2252 x1000

Mail: 800 N. Magnolia Ave., #105
        Orlando, FL 32803

As I mentioned in the foreword, I wrote this book to help you get a better understanding of your responsibilities and get you going on track to better plan management. In that regard, I hope this book has helped you. We can always be reached directly for inquires, but we are also willing to talk to other advisors, attorneys, or anyone else who may need some guidance, to the extent that our schedules permits.

We wish you the very best of success managing your plan, and we're here to help if we can!

ABOUT THE AUTHOR

Andrew Dickens is a native Floridian, born and raised on the east coast of Florida. He is the oldest of five adopted boys. He graduated high school in Volusia County and went to college in the state of Florida. After working in marketing shortly after school, he was re-introduced to his former high school classmate Thelma and they were married two years later. They have two daughters, Ariel and Keira. They live in Volusia County, close to their extended family.

Before joining Summit Wealth Partners, Inc., Andrew worked with the John Hancock Financial Network and Signator Investors Inc. Andrew is a wealth advisor for Summit Wealth Partners, Inc. He focuses on retirement and estate planning, business succession planning, and retirement plan consultation. Andrew is passionate about integrating those areas to produce best possible outcomes, and came to Summit Wealth Partners Inc. to enhance and apply those skills with their clients. He currently holds the Series 7, Series 6, and Series 66 securities licenses, and the 2-15 Florida life, health and variable contracts license.

Andrew is an authority on defined contribution planning and Employee Retirement Income Security Act (ERISA) fiduciary matters. His experience has taught him that employers need more help than they often realize, and he strives to deliver a service model to his clients that few in the industry are currently using. He believes that retirement plan advisors need broaden their scope of services to fulfill a larger role in managing their clients' needs, escaping beyond just the fiduciary investment advisor into a more holistic "shepherd or quarterback" style of service.

He believes strongly in the need for sensible legislative and regulatory initiatives to get more employers onboard with offering retirement plans, thereby getting more American workers access to the savings benefits these plans provide. He believes this should be done by educating and incentivizing the business community, not by compelling them. He also strongly believes in the call for greater fee transparency for all levels of service to help employers get a firm grasp of the headwinds that the plan and its participants are facing.

When he's not working, Andrew enjoys spending time with his family going on trips to the beach, camping, kayaking, fishing, barbecuing and watching football and soccer.

ACKNOWLEDGMENTS
AND RESOURCES

I owe my professional development and education in this industry to most, if not all of the companies and individuals listed in this section and in the bibliography, and I would be remiss not to credit them for their efforts in helping us learn, grow, and protect the industry and our businesses.

I've included U.S. legal code, IRS guidelines, legal opinions, case law, best practices, industry insights, relevant news, and more. Some of the information I have relayed was of my own design, but most of it is a conglomeration of best practices and insights that have been floating around the industry for years. Some of it was taught, and some of it was borrowed, and some of it was altered to fit the discussion.

All of the contributors on the following pages are great sources of information and other resources; take advantage of them!

A

ABG	www.abgncs.com/
ADP	www.adp.com/
Alliance Bernstein	www.alliancebernstein.com/
Allianz	www.allianzlife.com/
American Beacon	www.americanbeaconfunds.com/
American Century	corporate.americancentury.com/en.html
American Funds	www.americanfunds.com/
Ameritas	www.ameritas.com/wps/portal/corp
Ascensus	www.ascensus.com/
ASPPA	www.asppa.org/

B

Bates and Company, Inc.	www.batesco.com/
Blackrock	www.blackrock.com/
Blue Star Retirement Services	www.bluestarretirementservices.com/
BMO Financial Group	www.bmo.com/home
BNY Mellon	www.bnymellon.com/
BPAS, Inc.	www.bpas.com/
Business Transition Advisors	www.businesstransitionadvisors.com/

C

Calvert Investments	www.calvert.com/
Carpenter Morse Group	www.carpentermorse.com/
Center for Due Diligence	www.thecfdd.com/home
Charles Schwab	www.schwab.com/
Columbia Management	www.columbiamanagement.com/
Commonwealth Financial Network	www.commonwealth.com/
CUNA Mutual	www.cunamutual.com/

D

Delaware Investments	www.delawareinvestments.com/
Department of Labor	www.dol.gov/
Drinker Biddle	www.drinkerbiddle.com/

E

Eaton Vance	www.eatonvance.com/
ERISA Fiduciary Administrators	www.erisafiduciaryadministrators.com/

F

Federated Investors	www.federatedinvestors.com/FII/home.do

Fidelity	www.fidelity.com/
Franklin Templeton	www.franklintempleton.com/
F-Squared Investments	f-squaredinvestments.com/

G

Goldman Sachs	www.goldmansachs.com/
Great West	www.greatwest.com/
Guardian	www.guardianlife.com/index.htm

I

Invesco	www.invesco.com/portal/site/global
Internal Revenue Service	www.irs.gov/
Ivy Funds	www.ivyfunds.com/

J

Janus	www.janus.com/
JP Morgan	www.jpmorgan.com/pages/jpmorgan
John Hancock	www.johnhancock.com/

K

Kravitz Inc.	www.kravitzinc.com/

L

Lincoln Financial Group	www.lfg.com/

M

Manning & Napier	www.manning-napier.com/
Martin, Martin and Randall	www.mmrplans.com/
MassMutual	www.massmutual.com/
Mesirow	www.mesirowfinancial.com/
Metlife	www.metlife.com/
MFS Investment Management	www.mfs.com/
Milliman Investments	us.milliman.com/solutions/investment/
Morningstar	www.morningstar.com/

N

NAPA	www.napa-net.org/
Nationwide	www.nationwide.com/
Natixis	ngam.natixis.com/global/1250194644819/Home
Neuberger-Berman	www.nb.com/_layouts/www/index.aspx
Newport Group	www.newportgroup.com/
New York Life	www.newyorklife.com/
Nuveen Investments	www.nuveen.com/Home/Default.aspx

O

One America	www.oneamerica.com/
Oppenheimer	www.opco.com/

P

Pacific Life	www.pacificlife.com/
PAi	www.pai.com/
Paychex	www.paychex.com/
Pension Resource Institute	www.pension-resources.com/
Pentegra Retirement Services	www.pentegra.com/
Pete Swisher	401kfiduciarygovernance.com/
PIMCO	www.pimco.com/Pages/default.aspx
Plan Advisor	www.planadviser.com/
Plan Sponsor	www.plansponsor.com/
PNC	www.pnc.com/
Principal Financial Group	www.principal.com/index.shtm
Prudential/Mullin TBG	www2.mullintbg.com/
Putnam	www.putnam.com/

R

Retirement Plan Specialists, Inc.	www.wehelppeopleretire.com/
Ridgeworth	www.ridgeworth.com/

S

Social Security Administration	www.ssa.gov/
Stadion	www.stadionmoney.com/stadionmoney/start

T

TD Ameritrade	www.tdameritrade.com/
Thornburg Investment Management	www.thornburginvestments.com/
TIAA-CREF	www.tiaa-cref.org/public/index.html
TRA	tra401k.com/
Transamerica	www.transamerica.com/individual/
T. Rowe Price	corporate.troweprice.com/ccw/home.do

V

VALIC	www.valic.com/
Voya/ING	voya.com/

W

Wagner Law Group	www.wagnerlawgroup.com/
Wilmington Trust	www.wilmingtontrust.com/wtcom/

BIBLIOGRAPHY

American Institute of CPAs. (2010). Plan Investments in Bank Collective Investment Funds. *AICPA Employee Benefit Plan Audit Quality Center.*

American Society of Pension Professionals and Actuaries. (2012). *Plan Financial Consulting Part 2 Study Guide, 1st Ed.* Arlington: ASPPA.

Baker, J., & Abbey, D. (2009). A Fiduciary by Any Other Name...Thoughts on Properly Delegating Fiduciary Duties. *Benefits Law Journal*, Vol. 22, No. 1.

Brown, Andy. (2014). *Chefs Who Don't Eat Their Own Cooking.* Retrieved from Brown Wealth Management, LLC: www.brownwm.com/chefs-dont-eat-cooking/

Center for Due Diligence. (2009). *Fiduciary Liability and E&O Insurance for ERISA Plans: Most Don't Have It.* Western Springs: CFDD.

Dacey, D. R. (2010). *Fiduciary Duty and Timeliness of 401(k) Participant Deposits.* WithumSmith+Brown, PC .

DiCarlo, P., & Hootkins, E. (2014). Labor Department Disclosure Compliance Is Key to Turning Off Plan Fee Litigation. *Pension and Benefits Daily.*

Employee Benefits Security Administration. (2003). *Small Pension Plan Audit Waiver Regulation.* Retrieved from United States Department of Labor: www.dol.gov/ebsa/faqs/faq_auditwaiver.html

Employee Benefits Security Administration. (2004). *Understanding Retirement Plan Fees and Expenses.* Retrieved from United States Department of Labor: www.dol.gov/ebsa/publications/undrstndgrtrmnt.html

Employee Benefits Security Administration. (2006, May). *Voluntary Fiduciary Correction Program.* Retrieved from United States Department of Labor: www.dol.gov/ebsa/newsroom/fs2006vfcp.html

Employee Benefits Security Administration. (2010). *Meeting Your Fiduciary Responsibilities.* Retrieved from United States Department of Labor: www.dol.gov/ebsa/publications/fiduciaryresponsibility.html

Employee Benefits Security Administration. (2012). *Final Regulation Relating to Service Provider Disclosures Under Section 408(b)(2).* Retrieved from United States Department of Labor: www.dol.gov/ebsa/newsroom/fs408b2finalreg.html

Employee Benefits Security Administration. (2014). *Fact Sheet: EBSA Achieves Over $1.6 Billion in Total Monetary Results in Fiscal Year 2013.* Retrieved from United States Department of Labor: www.dol.gov/ebsa/newsroom/fsFYagencyresults.html

Employee Benefits Security Administration. (n.d.). *Delinquent Filer Voluntary Compliance Program.* Retrieved from United States Department of Labor: www.dol.gov/ebsa/newsroom/0302fact_sheet.html

Employee Benefits Security Administration. (n.d.). *Employee Retirement Income Security Act.* Retrieved from United States Department of Labor: www.dol.gov/compliance/laws/comp-erisa.htm

Employee Benefits Security Administration. (n.d.). *Form 5500 Series.* Retrieved from United States Department of Labor: www.dol.gov/ebsa/5500main.html

Employee Benefits Security Administration. (n.d.). *Guidance on Settlor v. Plan Expenses.* Retrieved from United States Department of Labor: www.dol.gov/ebsa/regs/AOs/settlor_guidance.html

Employee Benefits Security Administration. (n.d.). *Prohibited Persons.* Retrieved from United States Department of Labor: www.dol.gov/ebsa/oemanual/cha47.html

Employee Benefits Security Administration. (n.d.). *Selecting An Auditor For Your Employee Benefit Plan.* Retrieved from United States Department of Labor: www.dol.gov/ebsa/publications/selectinganauditor.html

Employee Benefits Security Administration. (n.d.). *The Employee Retirement Income Security Act (ERISA).* Retrieved from United States Department of Labor: www.dol.gov/compliance/laws/comp-erisa.htm

Glass, R. (2012). *Articles and Papers Written.* Retrieved from Investment Horizons: www.investmenthorizons.com/Papers_401(k)_Fiduciary_Checklist.PDF

Glass, R. (2013). 401(k) Plans May Be Sitting Ducks: Will Regulations Compel DC Fiduciaries to Examine Their Own Conflicts of Interest? *Pension and Investments.*

Goodwin Procter. (2012). Sixth Circuit Holds That ERISA Preempts State Law Claims Against Nonfiduciary Plan Custodian. *ERISA Litigation Update.*

Grantz, J., & Samford, M. (n.d.). Deconstructing the Discretionary Fiduciary Models: ERISA Section 3(38) Investment Managers vs. Discretionary Trustees.

Halpern, S. (2014). *Role of the Independent Fiduciary.* Arthur J. Gallagher and Co.

Internal Revenue Service. (2014). *401(k) Plan Fix-It Guide.* Retrieved from IRS: www.irs.gov/Retirement-Plans/401(k)-Plan-Fix-It-Guide

Internal Revenue Service. (2014). *Are Your Social Security Benefits Taxable?* Retrieved from IRS: www.irs.gov/uac/Newsroom/Are-Your-Social-Security-Benefits-Taxable

Internal Revenue Service. (2014). *Form 5500 Corner.* Retrieved from IRS: www.irs.gov/Retirement-Plans/Form-5500-Corner

Internal Revenue Service. (2014, Oct). *Retirement Topics - Contributions.* Retrieved from IRS: www.irs.gov/Retirement-Plans/Plan-Participant,-Employee/Retirement-Topics-Contributions

Internal Revenue Service. (2014, Feb). *Roth IRAs.* Retrieved from IRS: www.irs.gov/Retirement-Plans/Roth-IRAs

Jackson, C., Kallstrom, D. W., & Martin, A. (2010). *Who May Sue You and Why: How to Reduce Your ERISA Risks, and the Role of Fiduciary Liability Insurance.* Warren: Chubb Group of Insurance Companies.

Jones, D., Ziga, K., & Chong, S. (n.d.). ERISA Fiduciary Responsibility and Liability. Dechert LLP.

Kastrinsky, S. (2005). *ERISA Section 404(c) and Investment Advice: What is an Employer or Plan Sponsor to Do?*

KCG Consultant Group, I. (2010). *Policy, Process and Procedure - What's the Difference?* Retrieved from KCG Consultant Group, Inc.: kcggroup. com/PoliciesProcessesProcedureDifferences

Kravitz, D., Guidroz, K., & Sansone, S. (2010). *Beyond the 401(k).* Encino: Kravitz Publishing.

Legal Information Institute. (n.d.). *29 U.S. Code § 1001 - Congressional findings and declaration of policy.* Retrieved from Cornell University Law School: www.law.cornell.edu/uscode/text/29/1001

Mercado, D. (2014). 401(k) fiduciary lawsuit raises questions on record keeping. *Investment News.*

Moore, R. (2014, Sept). *Signature Authority May Trigger ERISA Fiduciary Status* . Retrieved from PlanAdviser: www.planadviser.com/Signature_ Authority_May_Trigger_ERISA_Fiduciary_Status.aspx

Muir, D., & Stein, N. (2013). Two Hats, One Head, No Heart: The Anatomy of the ERISA Settlor/Fiduciary Distinction.

Reish, F., & Faucher, J. (n.d.). *The Fiduciary Duty to Ask for Help.* Reish, Luftman, Reicher, and Cohen.

Reish, F., & Santagate, F. (2003). 401(k) INVESTMENTS: Satisfying ERISA's Fiduciary Rules. *CIMA: Building Profits.*

Roberts, J., & Treichel, B. (n.d.). *Fiduciary Governance: Challenges and Opportunities.* Pension Resource Institute.

Rosenbaum, A. (2013). *The Worthlessness of the 401(k) Fiduciary Warranty.* Garden City: The Rosenbaum Law Firm P.C.

Scalia, L. A., & Jacobson, J. (2013). 2014 Planning for ERISA single-employer defined contribution plan operations. *FYI- In Depth*, Vol. 36, Issue 94.

Simoneaux, S. (2012). *Retirement Plan Consulting for Financial Professionals, 4th Edition.* Arlington: ASPPA.

St. Martin, A. (2005). *Fiduciary Issues in ERISA-Covered Plans.* Groom Law Group.

Swisher, P. (n.d.). *15 Misconceptions About the Three Principal Fiduciary Roles in a Retirement Plan.* Pentegra Retirement Services.

Swisher, P. (2012). *401(k) Fiduciary Governance: An Advisors Guide.* Arlington: ASPPA.

Swisher, P. (n.d.). Stupid Investment Tricks: Interesting, Risky, or Downright Dumb Retirement Plan Investments. *Journal of Pension Benefits.*

The Oyez Project. (2009). *LARUE v. DEWOLFF, BOBERG & ASSOCIATES, INC.* Retrieved from The Oyez Project at IIT Chicago-Kent College of Law: www.oyez.org/cases/2000-2009/2007/2007_06_856

Uniform Law Commission. (n.d.). *Prudent Investor Act Summary.* Retrieved from Uniform Law Commission: www.uniformlaws.org/ActSummary.aspx?title=Prudent%20Investor%20Act

United States Department of Labor. (1996). *EBSA Final Rules.* Retrieved from United States Department of Labor: www.dol.gov/ebsa/regs/fedreg/final/96_14093.pdf

Wagner Law Group. (n.d.). *Fiduciary Status: Understanding the Different Roles and Status of 401(k) Fiduciaries.* Blackrock.

Wagner, M. (2010). *A Plan Sponsor's Fiduciary Duties Under ERISA: With Great Responsbility Comes Great Potential Liability.* Wagner Law Group.

Wagner, M. (n.d.). Case suggests that RFPs may be necessary to fulfill fiduciary duties. *401(k) Advisor.*

Wagner, M., Migausky, S., & Blynn, D. (2012). *The ERISA Fiduciary Compliance Guide.* Erlanger: The National Underwriting Company.

William Gallagher Associates. (n.d.). *What Can Noncompliance Cost You?* William Gallagher Associates.

www.ingramcontent.com/pod-product-compliance
Lightning Source LLC
Chambersburg PA
CBHW060406220326
41598CB00023B/3041